A LOVE SO FORBIDDEN THAT ONLY GOD CAN UNDERSTAND

T.J. EDWARDS

A Love So Forbidden Only God Can Understand
Copyright © 2020 by T.J. Edwards
978-1-7361106-9-0

Copyright notice: All rights reserved under the International and Pan-American Copyright Conventions. No part of this book may be reproduced or transmitted in any form or by any means, electronic or mechanical, including photocopying and recording, or by any information storage and retrieval system, without permission in writing from publisher.

This is a work of fiction. Names, places, characters, and incidents are either the product of the author's imagination or are used fictitiously, and any resemblance to any actual persons, living or dead, organizations, events, or locales is entirely coincidental.

Warning: the unauthorized reproduction or distribution of this copyrighted work is illegal. Criminal copyright infringement, including infringement without monetary gain, is investigated by the FBI and is punishable by up to 5 years in prison and a fine of $250,000.

For more information, email tjpublicationspresents@gmail.com.

This book is dedicated to the struggles, indescribable pains and sacrifices that both myself and my incredible wife have gone through in order to be together. Jelissa Shante Edwards, I love you, I honor you, and you will always be my purpose. You are my life. These truths, though you have live them beside me are for you first, and then the world

This book is also dedicated to my sister and one of my strongest supporters, Ms. Catina Lester. I appreciate you, Queen. You already know our struggles are real, but we conquer them day by day as only us project kids can. Much love and appreciation.

CALLING ALL ASPIRING AUTHORS!

T & J PUBLICATIONS PRESENTS is NOW accepting submissions in the following genres; street lit, urban romance, paranormal romance, contemporary romance.

Please submit the first three chapters of your **properly formatted (12pt font)**, **completed** manuscript along with the synopsis to: tjpublicationspresents@gmail.com, ensuring that the subject line is the author's name and book's title. Submissions must be in a word document. Submissions will be rejected if guidelines are not adhered to. Response time is 48-72 hours. If you submit a completed 3-part series and it is accepted by TJP, an *advance will be offered.

Advance amount TBD

CHAPTER 1
HOUSE OF PAIN

*"In this world, there are two types of pain:
pain that hurts you and pain that changes you."*

"Deborah! Deborah! Where the fuck you at? Bring yo' ass here right now!" My father snapped, before he took a long swallow of his Korbel brown liquor. He staggered slightly, and smiled for a bright second, then his smile turned into a mask of fury. "Dis bitch thank I'm playing wit' her. Bitch, where you at?" My father stood at five feet seven inches tall and built like a heavyweight boxer. In fact, he had been a golden glove boxer all throughout college. That was until he was shot several times within the cold-hearted streets of Chicago, Illinois where we lived.

My mother came out of the bathroom literally one minute after he'd started calling her. She had a drying towel wrapped around her body, and a plastic shower cap over her head. Her long natural curls sailed down her back and stopped just above her waist. "Baby, baby, baby, I was coming. I had to get the soap out of my eyes. My mother was five feet five inches tall, light-skinned with brown eyes, and strong Cherokee features. The African and Native American mixture transformed into beauty that often caused my father to become beyond insecure. His insecurities led him to become violent and verbally insulting.

My father burped and hiccupped, then pointed at her. "Where the fuck you been, bitch? Huh? And why you all the sudden taking a shower before I get home? You cheating on me?" Spit flew out of his mouth and landed on his chin.

My mother dropped her head as if she knew what was to come next, and she had to find a way to mentally prepare for it. "Alvin, I just wanted to relax. I thought you should have been home hours ago, but when I saw that you still weren't here, I got into the shower to chill out. Come on now, you should already know that I would never cheat on you. I would never risk our family for carnal pleasures." She raised her head to look at him. "Are you hungry? Your food is still in the oven. I can warm it up for you?"

He took a long swallow from his bottle and nodded. "Yeah bitch, I guess you can do that real good for me then, cause as soon as I'm done eating, I'm finna whoop yo' muthafuckin' ass." He licked around the rim of his bottle and frowned.

My three siblings and I laid on the floor in the living room on a pallet that my mother made for us. Financially, we were strapped for cash, and by strapped, I mean we were dirt poor. There was only one mattress inside of the house and it was located inside of my parents' bedroom. While they seemed to sleep soundly around her, I grew nervous at the fact that my father had just told my mother he was about to beat her after she'd fed him. I was ten years old at the time and had grown to understand that whenever he said that he was going to hurt somebody, especially one of us in the home, there was a guarantee that he was going to do it. My mother was just healing from the broken ribs he'd handed down to her in one of his many drunken rages. She often complained about the pain she felt every time she took a deep breath, and every time she did so, I felt sick to my stomach.

She paused after taking two steps into the kitchen. "So, you mean to tell me that you're going to beat me even if I haven't done anything wrong?" She never dared to look into his eyes that were shielded by bifocal glasses.

He finished his bottle and attempted to throw it into the garbage can. He missed. The bottle hit the rim of the garbage and crashed to the floor. The noise woke up both my brothers and sister. "Awright den, I ain't even gotta eat before I kick yo' ass. Guess I gotta build up some hunger anyway." He stepped into the kitchen with his fist balled.

My mother's eyes bucked. She backed up and wound up bumping into the small refrigerator that had come with the rundown Cabrini Green Project apartment. A box of cereal fell to the floor and spilled out it's cheap Aldi contents all over. "Please, Alvin. Don't do this. I haven't done anything wrong. I just wanna feed you and make sure you are good. Please, don't do this."

He stood looking at her for a long moment. "Come here, bitch." I could feel myself shaking worse than ever. My heart pounded in my chest. I got to my knees and dared to stand up. I could already imagine what was about to take place. I elbowed my oldest brother, Deion. "Bruh, get up. You gotta come with me in here and stop daddy from beating mama. The last time, he almost killed her."

Demon smacked his lips. "Man, that ain't got nothing to do with me. That's his woman. He is supposed to be beating her ass. Besides, I am only thirteen. He grown as hell. I ain't got no win with that nigga. He boxes and all of that crazy shit." He laid back down and fluffed his pillow that was made from a bunch of shirts that needed to be washed. "On top of that, my birthday coming up and I need some new gear. Pops the only one that can buy it. Moms broke as hell."

I mugged him. "So, you just finna let him beat on her while you sleep? Really? What type of son are you?" I was so angry that

I felt like punching him in the jaw, but he'd already whooped me multiple times. I was too weak, and he'd already been blessed with his teenage muscles that I had yet to get, so I decided against that.

"Fuck her, my nigga, damn. That ain't got nothing to do with me, or you. Ain't you tired of him whooping yo' ass for trying to protect her!" He laid flat on his back and closed his eyes. "Leave me the fuck alone."

Smack! Smack! Whoom!

My sister, Marie, started screaming at the top of her lungs. My heart sank. I dared to look into the kitchen. My mother was on the floor bleeding from the mouth, both of her feet kicking whilst her eyes rolled into the back of her head. Alvin stood over her. "Get up, bitch! Get up! You wanna cheat on me? Huh? Get the fuck up!" He grabbed a handful of her hair and made her stand up on wobbly legs. Blood dripped from her mouth.

She staggered, "I'm sorry, baby. I'm so sorry. "

Alvin pushed her back hard and punched her directly in the nose. She flew backwards into the refrigerator and slid down it with her eyes wide open. "You wanna cheat on me cause you fine? Huh, bitch! All my life you've been putting me through this shit." He flipped the table and roared like an angry beast. He bent over and took a hold of her hair again.

I jumped up on ten-year-old legs and ran into the kitchen without even thinking about the dire consequences. I jumped on his back and tightened my arms around his neck. "Leave her alone, daddy! Please, she didn't do anything wrong." Tears sailed down my cheeks and ran down into my shirt. I could hear him gag.

He backed all the way up into the corner of the door frame of the kitchen and slammed me into it as hard as he could. It poked into my spine, and I felt tingles shooting all up and down my body. I loosened my grips a bit, but then remembered my mother and tightened it all over again. He wasn't done with me just yet. He reached behind himself and took a hold of me. As soon as he had a good grip, he flipped me over his head and slammed me right on top of the table that was laying on its side.

I hollered out in pain as I felt three of my ribs crack one after the other. "Aww, pops!" Were the only words I managed to get out before the air felt like it was sucked out of me.

He ripped his shirt from his body. "Oh, so you wanna be the child to save this bitch? You think you man enough to come at me? Huh?" He grabbed me up and threw me into the wall. I fell back to the floor, crying silently. Even at that age, I refused to ever let him hear me whimper. "Get up, lil' nigga."

My mother woke up. She used the wall to help her come to her feet. Her mouth and nose dripped blood. Her eyes were watery. She swallowed and fell to her knees, clasped her hands together in a prayer like fashion and looked up to him. "Please, don't hurt him. He's just a child. He didn't know what he was doing, please Alvin."

Alvin took one step back and came forward with sheer quickness. He kicked her right in the face. She spit out her two front teeth and fell to the floor, losing consciousness. He dared to stomp her two times before he snatched me up and body slammed me. "I'ma teach yo' lil' ass." With that said, he proceeded to punch me so many times that I passed out coughing on my own blood.

When I woke up, I found myself in Cook County Hospital with an IV inside of my arm and all types of things hooked up to me. I started to panic and screamed for my mother who I was sure my father had killed.

Alvin rushed to my hospital bed and placed his hand over my mouth, this was after removing my oxygen mask. "Look here, you lil' bitch ass nigga, shut the fuck up before I kill you. If these white folks even think about locking me up, I'm killing everybody in that household. Now, shut up. Yo' mama is fine. I told the police that we got robbed coming from the Show. Stick to the script or else." He wrapped his hands around my neck and choked me for what felt like thirty seconds then he walked away from the bed after stuffing my mask into my face.

    I waited for a while to speak. I had to gather myself. "Where is she? Where is my mother, Pops?" He waved at me to be quiet, and then wiped his mouth with the back of his hand. She's in ICU, but that bitch is strong. She'll be okay. Take yo' lil' ass back to sleep. "

    There was no way I could do that. I was far too worried about my vulnerable mother. I was sure that he had killed her once and for all. But by the grace of God, he had not. She was forced to stay in the hospital for two weeks, and then they released her. Alvin was there front and center with a bouquet of roses. When the nurse wheeled her out into the parking lot and turned to walk away, us children watched from the family station wagon as he apologized and swore, he would never do it again.

    My mother's face was still swollen. One of her eyes, still closed, watered as she took him back, allowing for him to hug and kiss all over her. I remember being so confused. So lost and disgusted. How could a woman allow for a man to cause her so much pain and she continues to return to him time and time again? I didn't get it.

    I also didn't get how any man could love a woman so hard that it would cause him to beat her senseless and keep her as a regular at the hospital. I didn't understand how he could beat and torment his children the way that he did either. There were so many things that I did not understand as a ten-year-old kid, and even to this day as a grown man. But one thing was for certain and it was that I knew my life was going to go through a period of darkness before there could ever be any light.

    Deion placed his arm around my neck. "You see, that's why you should never try and save a bitch, cause she gon' always go back to that nigga. You'd be just wasting yo' time." He sat back and pulled his headphones over his head while I continued to watch my parents display affection toward one another.

    You see, women, when you allow for a man to verbally, physically, and mentally abuse you in front of your children, you are sending the message to your daughter that this is how a woman is supposed to be treated. That this is love. You instill lies of love into her mental software and your unintentional lessons become the standard to which she accepts as the norm. The weaker you are, the higher the probability that upon witnessing your endeavors, your daughter will be also.

When it comes to your son, he will think that this is the proper way to behave with his woman, shit, because this is what you allowed. As children, the greatest teachers are never those outside of the household but inside. The parents, especially the mother, is the greatest teacher of all, second to the father, or father figure.

The scene that played before my eyes left me emotionally scarred. I felt sick, weak, and distraught. I wanted to hate my mother yet love her at the same time. I started to believe that this was normal behavior for parents to behave in such a way. That my brother Deion was right. I needed to mind my own business, but then it happened...

CHAPTER 2
THE CLOSET

"My worst enemy has always been my memory."

"Please Alvin! Please, don't do it! Please, you are killing that boy!" My mother screamed as she tried her best to pry his hands from around my neck.

I couldn't breathe. My eyes bugged out of my head. I was shaking so bad that my teeth were chattering. "Get the fuck back, Deborah, or I swear by Allah that yo' ass gon' be next. He wanna fuck in my bidness, then I'ma show him where that's going to get him." As he said this, spit flew out of his mouth and landed on my forehead. He squeezed harder and harder. The world began to fade away and I couldn't honestly say that I didn't care.

At the age of thirteen, I felt like I was ready to die. I was tired of living, especially within our household. I was sick and tired of watching my father beat my mother to the point that she was forced to visit the hospital every other week and on top of that, there had been new developments within our household that caused me to nearly have a nervous breakdown, hence the reason my father was currently battering me.

My sister, Marie, ran into the living room with just a sheet wrapped around her. Only minutes prior, I'd caught our father on top of her, humping her waist, while she bit into a pillow and begged for him to get off her. My mother cried on the side of the bed, rocking back and forth whilst my father had his way with my ten-year-old sister as if she were not his blood, but a grown woman.

He broke my nose and stood up. "You bitch ass lil' nigga, that ought to learn you." He grabbed my ankle and drug me down the hallway and stuffed me inside of the small closet that was often infested with both rats and cockroaches that were so big you had to step on them twice before they stopped moving.

He kicked me multiple times, and stomped me four times, before closing the closet door and locking it with a combination lock. The entire time, I could hear my mother and sister begging him to let me out, to which he ignored them. Instead, he kept me locked inside of the closet for two straight days with no food and nothing to drink for the entire first day. On the second day, he came by five times and poured a cup of water under the door. I was forced to sip it off the ground. The water mixed with the blood that occasionally dripped from my face gave a taste of copper in my mouth, but I had to do what I had to do.

The day he released me, I was so weak that my mother had to carry me from the closet and into the bathroom where she helped me to sink into a hot bath. She washed me from head to toe and fed me. I threw everything that she did serve, back up and passed out. I woke up in the emergency room. I passed back out. The next time I opened my eyes, I was back home with my mother knelt beside me with tears in her eyes.

She shook her head front right to left. "All of this is my fault, son." She sniffed and hung her head low. "The only reason your father is doing these things to you is because of my sins. You shouldn't be going through this. "

As a young man, I always hated to hear my mother cry or whimper. These were the worst sounds that my ears could consume. I sat up and tried to look strong. My face was swollen. Both eyes were barely open, and it hurt when I breathed in or out, and at the same time my jaw hurt on both sides. "Mama, you good. Don't let my father allow for you to blame yourself for his mistakes. This ain't on you."

She nodded. "When it comes to him hurting you, yes, it is." She dropped her head. "Baby, there are things about me and Alvin that you don't know about, and I don't know how to tell you either." We sniffled. "I swear to God this man is going to kill one or the both of us one day."

"I don't care about him killing me. I just don't want him to hurt you no more. I don't care if he beat me a million times, as long as he never lays a finger on my mother again. I hate him so much, mama."

She placed her finger to her split lip and looked over her shoulder toward the open door to their bedroom. She hopped up and closed it. Even though my father wasn't even in the city at this time, he had her so traumatized that she still took the necessary precautions to ensure he couldn't hear us. She came back and knelt beside the bed where I laid on my back. "Don't ever use the word hate. Whenever you utter the word out of your mouth it gives place to the devil."

At thirteen, I felt like we were already living with the devil. I didn't care about giving place to him. I hated Alvin. I needed to let that be known. "Mama, why do you keep going back to dude? Why don't you leave?"

"Shoot boy, where I'ma go? Don't nobody want a woman with four kids. I have stretch marks and everythang. Shoot, I'm lucky yo' daddy still come home to me every night, well almost every night." She smiled weakly and grew weary.

I got off the bed and knelt beside her. "You don't need him, mama. You are strong enough to bounce and you can still make it. I wish you could see how beautiful you are. Don't nobody care about those stretch marks."

"Yes, they do. Alvin said those are the first thing a man looks at, and if you got them it causes the man to throw up. He also said that because I done gave birth to five children, my stuff down there ain't no good. He says it's too loose and that's why he needed Marie. He said it would be better for him to keep it in the family then outside of it." She grew quiet for a long while, then suddenly smiled. "Besides, I've been with him ever since I was fourteen and my mother kicked me out. I don't know nothin' 'bout nobody else. He all I know."

I guess when I looked at it from her point of view, I could see and understand where she was coming from. My mother got pregnant with Deion at the age of fourteen. My grandparents were devout Jehovah's Witnesses, and they had zero tolerance for teenage pregnancy. Upon finding out, they kicked my mother out of the house and into the streets. Alvin's mother, Gwen, took my mother in and turned a blind eye to everything that went on between her son and my mother while they lived under her roof.

Alvin was seventeen and my mother was fourteen. It didn't take long for him to brainwash her and for him to turn her into the woman that *he* had desired her to be. Over the next five years, she would give birth to five children and receive no schooling. She was forbidden to leave the house by him, since my grandmother Gwen. My sister, Gwenetta, had passed away shortly after my mother gave birth to her. Even though my mother had never been given the opportunity to spend a day with Gwenetta, she often spoke about her as if she'd always been with us.

She wrapped her arms around my neck and looked me in the eyes. I am not strong enough to leave him. He's all I know and the only man I could ever love. It's complicated. "She rubbed the side of my face. "Besides, that's grown folk's business. Don't you worry your heart 'bout me. I'm a Memphis girl. A little country with a whole lot of heart. I'll be alright." She kissed my cheeks again and fell back on her haunches.

"When you grow up, you make sure you never put your hands on a woman. Always treat her like a Queen, son, you know, the way that your father, or no man, has ever treated me." She shook her head. "Sometimes, when I hear about how men love women, and how they take the time out to cater to them, being romantic and thangs like that, I just know that it's all a fairy tale. It ain't real. Never once have I come across a man that cared for me in the way that they should have." She laughed, "I personally thank women are nothing more than a man's trash. At least, it's all that I know." She lowered her head for a while, and suddenly broke into tears. "Why do you love me so much? I am a horrible mother and a weak woman. I really don't understand why God even allowed for me to have breath in my body this long. I ain't nothing but filth."

I don't know why her words cut me so deep, but suddenly, I began to cry my eyes out. The tears poured down my face and the next thing I knew, I was holding my mother and squeezing her. I started to shake. It became hard for me to breathe. "Mama, you are perfect. It's my father that is not."

"No, I'm not either. I'm ugly. Ain't nobody 'round thanking I look like somethin', and once I takes my shirt off and they see my stretch marks, oh the thangs they gon' have to say 'bout me. The only person that wants me is your father, and the only human being that loves me in this world seems to be you. I don't even thank Marie loves me anymore, you know, now that he been jumping up and down inside of her and what not."

I only held her tighter. I felt sick to my stomach at the thought of my old man having sex with my little sister, but it was a constant reality around our home after I exposed it. He almost made it seem like Marie was the new replacement for my mother. Witnessing their displays of affection was enough to have made me lose my mind, and I am certain that a major part of me was lost back then because of the series of serious events that went on inside of our small Project apartment.

"Know what I wanna ask you son, huh?" She stood on her knees and walked forward until we were face to face. She stroked my cheek as she looked me in the eyes. "Do you wanna know?" She smiled that dimpled smile. The same dimples that she had passed down to me along with the high cheek bones and broad forehead.

"What mama? You can ask me anything." I was still shaking, wondering what our future held with a man like Alvin heading our household. Sick images and audio of him and Marie plagued my mind. I tried to think about so many other things, but none of them could wash away the poisonous thoughts that ate away at my innocence.

She leaned into my face and kissed me ever so lightly on the lips. "Guess, I just wanna know how it is that Marie can be so crazy about her daddy because of what they are doing and all, but you say you love me, but you ain't never tried to love me in the same way? How can you love yo' mama, yet you don't desire me enough to come into me? You're surely old enough now." She kissed me again, but this time she licked my lips ever so tenderly.

I moved my head backward. I swear I didn't believe what she'd just done, nor what it appeared that she was getting at. I stood up and looked down on her. She stood up with me. "Are you mad at me, son? Do you hate me now!" The way her eyes opened so wide it appeared to me as if she was close to having a mental breakdown. I didn't know what to do other than to comfort her.

"Mama, I don't hate you. I was just trying to understand what you were getting at. I'm too young to know, that's all. I'm only thirteen." I felt that if I reminded her of my age that it would help her to snap out of whatever it was that had her bound captive.

"I know, baby, but you're already so big and strong. Listen to me, I don't even know what I am saying. Never mind, T.J., just forget I even said anything." She hugged me close. "I feel like I am losing my mind. I am yearning for unconditional love. I am hungry to be desired. I need to know what it feels like to be desired and enamored by a man that loves me. I've never had that." She kissed me again. "I'm sorry, baby. Your mother is just broken." With that said, she walked out of the room and slammed the bathroom door.

Twenty minutes later, I found her on the bathroom floor with both of her wrists slit deeply. Alvin and Marie were just walking in the door all hugged up and Deion was right behind them. After Alvin slapped her around for a moment because in his words, she had been stupid. He rushed her to the hospital just in time.

They were able to save her and give her a blood transfusion. The doctor referred her to the psychiatric ward, and they came and got her that night and kept her for a week. During this week, Alvin beat me senseless every single day. By the time my mother came back, she needed to rush me to the hospital where they kept me and referred me to Chicago Protective Services. Before they could snatch me out of the home, Alvin told them that I had been jumped by a rival gang. When they found out that we lived in the Cabrini Green Project, they let the matter go and allowed me to go home with my family. The next two years would be the worst years of both mine and my mother's life.

CHAPTER 3
GUN CRAZY

"Your genetics load the gun. Your lifestyle pulls the trigger."
-Mehmet Oz

"Nigga, wake yo' ass up and get a load of this." When I opened my eyes, I saw Deion with a sawed-off shotgun pointed directly between the center of my eyes. I jumped backward. He laughed, "yeah nigga, this ma'fucka right here'll send a nigga straight to the morgue. Pops just gave it to me for my birthday." He took a step back and looked it over in admiration.

I scooted from under him and stood up. "Bruh, why every time you get a new gun you gotta put it in my face or you find some type of way to brandish it?" I was very irritated. First because I'd been up all night working at the Chicago Sun-Times newspaper depot, so I was pissed that he woke me up out of my sleep, but secondly, because this was the spring before my sixteenth birthday and already four of my friends had been brutally murdered by gun fire. Two of them had been killed right in front of me. This was early 2000 and the bangers within our city of Chicago were already dropping bodies left and right.

"I don't wanna talk about all of that. Get yo' ass up. The brothas wanna holler at you under the Ravenswood. It's time for you to come on home. "He tucked the shotgun into his Girbaud jeans and smiled evil like.

My mother must have been standing outside of the living room because when she walked in, she was already shaking her head. "No, no, no, this is not going to happen. He ain't joining some fucking gang, and he ain't going with you just so some lil' boys can beat him up."

Deion frowned. "You don't know shit about the street, so be yo' ass quiet 'fore I tell Pops to check yo' ass. Secondly, why you always trying to shield this nigga? You treat him like he a bitch. Like he Marie or something. This is Chicago. He gotta be plugged or they gon' plug his ass up."

"Deion, who do you think you talking to?" My mother stepped forward as if she were ready to discipline him. Deion pulled the shotgun out of his waistband and she jumped back. Her left eye was already blackened, and her bottom lip was swollen. "You know what, y'all gon' head and do whatever it is that you're going to do. This doesn't concern me anymore. "She turned around and walked away.

As soon as she was out of the vicinity, I jumped into Deion's face. "Say bruh, watch how you be talking to our mother. I don't care about that gun you toting. That shit was real foul." I wanted to bust him in the jaw to emphasize my point. I was sure that had I done that; he would have pulled the trigger with no remorse.

"Fuck what you talkin' 'bout, bruh. I ain't got no respect for another nigga's bitch. She always getting her ass whipped for some stupid shit she done did. I don't honor her or nobody else so fuck you. Get dressed. We headed to the fighting life. You got three of the lil' Moes to box in order to become a part of the mob. Good luck. Just know that if they whoop you, I'm killing you on site. Just as if you were a Pit Bull that lost in a fight. On the Five nigga, you gotta go down. Hurry up, I'll be downstairs."

After he left the room, I got up and got dressed. While to so many people reading this, I can tell that this whole ordeal may seem crazy or farfetched but it's not. It's sad to say that in the city of Chicago this was the norm. If you don't plug into the gangs that control your neighborhood, then your likelihood of surviving is basically skinny to none. I was ready, a bit fearful, but still ready, nonetheless.

When I got to the battlefield, my brother's Blackstone homies were already there posted up. They were about thirty deep and had formed a circle to complete the makeshift fighting arena. The name of his group was called the Almighty Black P. Stones. They were back then and still to this day, one of the deadliest gangs in the United States of America. They built its legacy from dirty money, betrayals, and bloodshed.

When they saw us approaching, all the members began nodding their heads. They opened the circle and allowed for us to step into it. Once inside, I was able to see my opponents. Three hefty shirtless teenagers that were known around the hood to be fighters. I didn't care. My father had whooped my ass so much by this point that I didn't think there was any dude my age that could stand up to my hand game. In addition to that, I hated myself so much that I yearned for the pain they were about to try and inflict upon me.

Deion turned his hat to the left side and hung a red bandanna out of his pocket. Let's get it Five."

Before they could devise their strategy of who was going to fight me first, I went into action. I rushed the biggest one and knocked his ass out with one hit, before I turned to my right and dropped the second one with three quick hooks. The third one jumped into the air and kicked me hard in the back. I flew forward and landed on my chest. He jumped on top of me and proceeded to plant me to the ground. He punched me repeatedly in the back of the head.

I struggled to get up but couldn't. I was trapped and growing dizzy. When Deion announced that we had to stand back up, I was so happy that I started to cry front anger and elation. Once we were on our feet, I rushed him and beat him easily. He outweighed me by fifty pounds wet, but the constant blows were no match. Twenty punches later, he was laid out on the ground snoring like the bear that he resembled. All the bangers embraced me and came off their hips to give me pistols. Right there, was the first time I had ever felt loved outside of my household.

Over the next year, I developed a hunger for guns, gang wars, and bloodshed. I got a rush from dropping the opposition. It made me feel a way when the opps held funerals for their members that my crew had dropped. It gave me a sense of peace and acceptance that I had never felt at home. Because of those feelings, I found myself lost in the life. I stayed on the frontlines of every gang war we were involved in and my name range bells all around the forte. They called me Ghost because I would slump an opp then be out of the vicinity before anybody could prove that I did it. I also had a knack for evading the enemy even when they were sure they had me cornered. I grew obsessed with murder and guns, and I knew it was only because deep down within my soul I was a broken boy.

The following eighteen months, I continued to experience abuse within my home, and I made the opps pay for my father's sins back out in the streets. I'm not proud of it. I caused a lot of bloodshed and dripped a bunch myself but at that time I felt like it was necessary. It was either get lost in the streets or blow my own head off after I killed Alvin, which is something I thought about doing every single day.

His drinking got worse and so did his drug usage. He'd taken to mixing crack with marijuana before he drank himself into an abusive state. During the times that he was under the influence, he would beat my mother so bad that afterwards she would be unrecognizable. This crushed me, and more and more, I began to plot his murder within my own mind. Before it could take effect, Alvin was arrested for a shooting that had been caught on camera. He was sent to the Cook County Jail where he was forced to come up with fifty thousand dollars for bail. While this should have been a time for rejoicing, that same month my mother was diagnosed with cervical cancer.

CHAPTER 4
PAIN AFTER THE UNTHINKABLE

"Pain changes people."

My mother, Deborah Lin Stevens-Edwards passed away on March 13, 2001, after having a horrific battle with cervical cancer. I'd watched my mother go from a nice one hundred- fifty pounds, all the way down to thirty-two pounds soaking wet. Four days before she passed away, and while on her deathbed, Deion had bailed Alvin out of jail, and Alvin had rushed to the hospital where he'd smacked my mother around one more time because she had been unable to get him out earlier.

I had been visiting my grandmother in the suburbs of Chicago at this time when I found out about it. I tore the city up looking for Alvin. My mind was made up. I was going to kill him. Before I could get the chance, he'd been apprehended by the authorities and held by the Marshalls pending federal weapons charges. They literally caught up to him thirty minutes after he beat her the final time. I was pissed because I wanted to send him to hell like I had so many other individuals that had caused me pain. I felt like the system had robbed me.

My mother's funeral was small, maybe twenty people. It was a very sad and naïve ceremony. I didn't cry. I couldn't. I was far too broken inside. Instead, I grabbed my guns and took to the streets living on a death wish. Instead of using precaution when I kicked off drama, I went kamikaze. I'd walk on the wrong block with guns in hand and just start blowing. I didn't care if I got hit or who I hit as long as it wasn't a child or a female. Any male was in jeopardy. All of them resembled my father to me. I took delight in watching them squirm on the pavement before I did whatever came to mind or retreated. I was a hungry, lunatic lion roaming the streets of Chicago with no regard and no mercy for an opp. I was lost.

Five months after my mother passed away and two juvenile stints later, I jumped into the dope game. Deion had plugged into some heavy hitters inside of the Moorish Science Temple of America, and they were bringing over fifty kilos of heroin a week from Libya. He changed his name to Ahmad and held a strong position with the Black P Stones as well. I climbed aboard, and by my nineteenth birthday, I had three hundred thousand dollars in cash tucked and a brand-new Jaguar sitting on twenty-four-inch Sprewell's, which ran me ten thousand for each rim.

Money came hand over fist often, and steadily. Everything seemed to be falling into place for the better, though I was still missing my mother like crazy. I took to smoking plenty purple haze and drinking Seagram's gin by the bottle to cope with my suicidal thoughts and depression. I still bussed my gun weekly and found shelter in blood shed.

It was the spring of my nineteenth birthday when I met the first female, I would feel some type of way about. Her name was Akia. She was five-feet-five inches tall, caramel, brown eyes, ghetto as hell, but she talked proper. She had long braids and was originally from Gary, Indiana. I had met her in Madison, Wisconsin while shopping at one of their many malls. Even though I hated myself, I loved dressing fresh, and I loved clothes and shoes. I had to have everything top of the line, and while Chicago was frivolous for long lines whenever Michael Jordan put out a new shoe, Madison was not. Every time he released a new pair, I traveled to Madison and copped every color.

This one particular day I was there with Ahmad, Akia approached him and told him that she wanted to get up with me, but she was too nervous to do so. Long story short, we got up with each other that day, and dated for four months before she got pregnant. We had a son. Our relationship was okay, puppy love. She was only seventeen, and I was a new nineteen. I was consumed with the streets. I showered her with expensive gifts, plenty money, jewelry, and cars but not a lot of my time. We argued a lot and before it started it was over. I didn't feel any way about it either. I was in love with the streets and fast money.

The summer of 2003 is when it all went downhill. I'll never forget it. It was me, Akia, her sister, Ranay, and my little brother, Gotto. We had just come from a nightclub that didn't card at the door. All of us were teenagers and had been drinking and smoking bud inside of this club. I had two bottles of Moët in my hand and I was drinking out of each one. Akia was mad at me because she had tried to drink out of one of the bottles and I had not allowed her to do it. I didn't like drinking behind nobody, not even my woman, and I didn't smoke behind anybody either. I had never had a disease in my life, and I wasn't trying to catch no Herpes and all that other stuff.

Anyway, Akia got rejected from trying to sip out of my bottle and started hollering about how she wanted me to take her home. I told her to go sit her ass down and to wait until I was ready. She snapped and said that she was ready to go right now. She was hollering and making a scene. I didn't care. I wasn't ready to go just yet, and I told her just that. She stormed away and I went back to the VIP section where my brother and her sister was. "Yo', Ranay, yo' sister bugging. Tell her to sit her ass down."

Ranay laughed. "I bet you wish you would have chosen me now, don't chu. Nigga, I would have been all up yo' fine ass, submissive as hell. It's too late now though. You got her pregnant, ugh." She shook her head in disgust.

My brother laughed. "Shorty, stop trying to get at Ghost. That shit foul as hell. That's your whole ass sister."

Ranay shrugged. "It's hard out here. That nigga be having stupid chips. She acts like she doesn't get it. He keeps her ass spoiled." She appeared jealous.

Akia walked up with two dudes, one I knew to be her ex. "Say Ghost, I'm ready to go. Blue gon' drive me home, you ain't gotta worry about it." She snatched her purse from beside me and rolled her eyes.

I stood up. Prior to this incident, about two months back, I had already whooped Blue for overstepping his bounds when it came to my pregnant child's mother. I was feeling like since the hands didn't teach him his lesson, maybe a slug would. "Say Blue, you on this bullshit again fuckin' wit' my business?"

He slipped his hand under his shirt and smiled. "I do what the fuck I wanna do. This my city and my old bitch. You better take that shit back to Chicago, my nigga, onna G." When he said this, three other dudes stepped from the crowd with their hats broke to the right.

My little brother backed away and left me. He pulled Ranay along with him. I laughed at his cowardice ass and then turned back to Blue. "You holding, huh? You strapped. That's your first gun? I busted up laughing with my heart beating fast. I grew angrier by the second.

He held the gun firmer. "I'm about to drop her off. If you don't want me to then suck my dick." As soon as the words left his mouth, I swung and broke his nose before dumping him on his neck. He dropped his gun. I picked it up and made his guys lay down. They were so pussy that two of them ran and the last one laid down. I stripped him and Blue right there in front of everybody and made the niggas leave the club ass naked. When we made it outside, we found my brother laid up against his car with two bullets in his shoulder. Had I not heard the sirens of the police, I had something vindictive on my mind for him as well for leaving me, but instead I helped him into the car and drove away.

    That night, me and Akia stayed up for three hours straight arguing about the situation. She insisted that it was my fault, and I didn't care what she was talking about. I felt that he had disrespected me in a major way and what had taken place was necessary. With that being said, I went to sleep, leaving her to deal with whatever she was feeling. It angered me because I truly felt that she was siding with her ex, and for as long as I had been back and forth from Chicago, Illinois to Madison, Wisconsin, a part of me felt like the two of them had something going on behind my back anyway. The feeling for me was always one of suspicion. When I opened my eyes the next morning, the entire bedroom was covered with police and that's when my next level of pain began.

CHAPTER 5
TEARS THAT NEVER CAME

"Waste no tears over the griefs of yesterday."
-Euripides

"Ahem, well, Mr. Edwards, it is clear after hearing all of the witnesses' testimonies and even the testimony from one of your own bloodline that you in fact are a menace to society. You took it upon yourself to batter and rob two men while holding them at gunpoint wiring an establishment that legally you were not supposed to be at. It is my understanding that you are not even from the state of Wisconsin, and that your record reflects that of violence and firearms back where you once resided within the state of Illinois. It seems to me that you just don't get it, but today I am going to make sure you do. You see, we are tired of you people from Illinois coming to Wisconsin to commit crimes and dirty up our state. None of you get the message, and I have been praying that I come face to face with one of you for such a time as this. With that said, under open air circumstances I would usually hand down a sentence of five years of total confinement, but as I stated before this is a special case."

He sat back and cracked his knuckles. An evil smile spread across his face. "Mr. Edwards, I'm going to use you as an example to show those where you come from to not come to Wisconsin for any reason other than the right reason. I am sentencing you to twenty years in prison plus fifteen years of extended supervision. A total of thirty-five years. You should be dead and gone by the time you get out. Good riddance." He slammed his gavel. "Next case!"

That night in my cell, I sat in silence and tried to force myself to cry. How were they expecting me to do twenty years in prison when I was only nineteen years old? When it was all said and done, I would be forced to complete more time locked up then I had on the streets. That just didn't make any sense to me. At the same time, I already knew I didn't even have *minimal* family support. I didn't have anybody. The only positive thing that I could come up with regarding my situation was the fact that Ahmad had already been sentenced to do time within the state of Wisconsin, so there was a good chance I would run into him somewhere down the line.

Other than that, I would be forced to do all this time on my own. I had to man up. And crying like a bitch wasn't in the cards for me. Tears were meant for the weak. When a man felt the need to cry, this is when he needed to inflict pain on another nigga that he felt was stronger than him. I couldn't allow for this situation to break me. Alvin had kept me locked inside of a closet in darkness, off and on throughout my entire childhood. It was like he had prepared me for such a time as this. I was ready, and I wasn't about to fold even in the least bit. I would do what I had to do to survive. And whatever that was, I would be with it.

So instead of getting on my knees and talking to God that night, I prayed up to my mother. "Yo moms, they got me. These devils tried their best to take my life, but I ain't finna cry. I'ma do what I gotta do, and if they kill me in the process of me doing whatever it takes, so be it. I miss you, and I thank you for your many sacrifices. I wish I could have sacrificed myself for you, and you could still be here. Thank you for being my hero." I did the sign of the crucifix over my body and hopped in my bed. I closed my eyes and smiled. Whatever my next journey was set to be, I promised to make it interesting.

CHAPTER 6

MY PAIN RUNS DEEP

"Hell is empty, and all the devils are here."
-William Shakespeare

I was sent to a double maximum-security prison called Columbia Correctional Institution. This was the same prison that was famous for housing Jeffrey Danger, the famous serial killer and the person that killed him. My first week there, three dudes got killed and two committed suicide. I was a bit nervous to be housed in such a place, but once again I had so much hate and anger inside of me that it blinded my commonsense.

The prison was painted a dirty purplish burgundy. It had no metal doors with two tiers full of yelling inmates, and officers inside of a big black bubble where they were supposed to protect you. I didn't see how they could get to a person in time if they were to have reached harm, and I don't think they cared that much either. The average time that a person was sentenced to at the facility was twenty years, and the most time a person had was six life sentences. They had purposely put me around all the dudes that had double life sentences or better. I guess this was to break me in. They were all from different locations within Wisconsin. They all seemed to hate those from Illinois. I was a target as soon as I opened my mouth and they asked me where I was from. Within ten days of getting off the bus, I found myself in the middle of a situation that was sure to cost me my life.

It was a Wednesday, just before nine in the morning. The inmates from my building had just been cleared to leave for the gymnasium. As we filed out one by one, I noticed that there was this big muscle-bound dude standing to the side of the doorway that everybody was coming out of. Every so often he would point to a dude and that person would step off to the side. He did this repeatedly until it was my time to come through the door. He pointed at me, but I kept going. I didn't know this nigga, and he didn't know me. I'd spent the last week trying to get a hold of my son's mother, but she was missing in action. I had all kinds of crazy stuff going through my mind regarding her and because I did, it had me short with everybody.

The big oaf stepped into my path. "Say lil' nigga, I know you are new here and all of that, but we run a system around dis ma'fucka. You ain't allowed to go to the gym unless you pay yo' dues. Since ain't no ma'fucka say you did, you ain't about to participate at rec. What type of family support you got?"

I looked this big ass nigga up and down and grew conscious of the fact that he was twice my size, and I had already heard it thought the grapevine that he had triple life for a bunch of murders. His name rang bells around the prison because he was a knockout artist. I filed all that information away and knew that it was still about to go down.

"Say my nigga, you don't know me to be asking me about my people. I don't give a fuck about your family, and I don't want you asking about me or mine. Second to that, I don't give a fuck how you stand on these niggas, but you ain't finna succeed on none of that with me." I started to walk past him again but this time, he stepped into my face.

Right away, he turned into Alvin. I cocked my head back and

brought it forward as fast and as hard as I could. My forehead connected with his nose and broke it. It snapped as loud as a twig in a quiet forest. He hollered out at the top of his lungs. I dropped to my knees and punched him with all my might right in the nuts. He doubled over holding his crotch. I straddled him and hit him over forty times, all face shots before the police pulled me off him. I was covered in blood and smiling as they drug me away.

They put me in the hole for three hundred days straight and kicked me out of the prison, saying I was too dangerous to be in their facility. They sent me east to a prison called Waupun Correctional Institution. This was the place where the long-term lifers were sent. Those that were merciless, rotten, cold hearted, and society had given up hope on. They placed me here just before my twentieth birthday. When the transport guard dropped me off, he shook his head and said, "Son, I'ma pray for you. I don't think you'll make it six months here before you are dead." I told him to watch me and fuck his prayers. I knew God didn't love me. I hated even the thought of somebody praying for me. I was hopeless.

I served six months in the hole from my infraction at Columbia. Their segregation consisted of a small closet like room with a toilet and sink. It was dirty, smelled terrible, and freezing cold. There were no windows or mirrors. You were not allowed hygiene or food other than the three meals a day they gave you. Suicides were happening every day, along with cell boxing; meaning that inmates screamed through the door at each other sending idiot threats of what was supposed to come once they saw one another in general population.

I stayed to myself and wrote my mother letters. I told her how beautiful she was, how much I missed her, and how important she was in my life. Then I would respond to my own letters how I thought she would. After I finished with the letters, my mind would start to wander.

The small room would get to me. I felt suffocated. It was

becoming harder to breath. I wanted to scream. My head started to spin. I started talking to myself and arguing with myself. Before the six months were finished, I had lost a bit more of my commonsense. I got out of the hole loony. The internal pain had manifested itself within the pits of my brain, and every so often because of the long segregation stint, I lost touch with reality every few minutes. It took me a couple months to snap out of this slight case of retardation. At least that's what I called it.

CHAPTER 7
THE DOMINANT LION

"Everyone wants to eat, but few are willing to hunt."
-MindsetOfABoss

One thing about prison, if you were fearless and had a crazy hand game, sooner or later all the so-called animals were going to back up off you. Within my first three months at Waupun, I had ten fights, and eight of them caused serious bloodshed. I was a complete predatory of men.

I sought out trouble before it came to me. Whenever I felt there was new opposition headed to my building, or one that I would have to worry about eventually, I went at them first. I didn't play any games, and I refused to take any losses. If I got whooped, that same dude had to fight me every day until I won as many battles between us as he did. While he and I were battling for supremacy, I took to whooping his guys whenever I found them lacking. After some time, I strengthened my stand-up game and became a force to be reckoned with.

Because I fought so much, I stayed in the hole a lot. It got to the point where they never even took my name tag off the door when I left the room in segregation because they knew I would be back. Instead of the hole being a place where I started to mentally deteriorate, it became my oasis. My time out from society within the prison. They never gave me less than six months to serve in the hole at a time, so whenever I was down there trapped in that little room, I had to be prepared to escape psychologically, which I did.

I started writing short stories to keep me entertained. My stories always included a stronger female lead that was hypersexual with the ability to mentally manipulate men before she crushed them in the most sadistic way. I don't know why but those stories made me happy. I started to write one after the other, and before I knew it, my time in the hole had expired. I would pack up my things and feel a sense of sadness as I was made to leave my place of refuge and most important, my writings.

Back in population, the reality of no family support swallowed me. I didn't have clothes, canteen, hygiene products, or none of the other luxuries that having financial support would award me. Life was super hard, and it made me severely depressed. Because I did not have any of these things, I sought to do my time in the hole because down there, everybody was even. Nobody could have anything more than what I had. As long as I couldn't see it, then it really didn't bother me.

I knew I was poor, and I knew I didn't have any family that loved me, so I hated myself. I hated my shadow. I hated anything that was associated with me. I would spend nights slapping myself in the face over and over until my lips bled. I remembered all the things Alvin said about me, believing him. On many nights, I wish I had a gun to kill myself. I just didn't want to be here any longer. I didn't see the point. It got so bad that I devised a plan to make the officers that ran the prison kill me. I was going to take one of them hostage and pull them outside under the armed tower where the officer inside of the tower would be forced to zoom into the scope on his thirty-thirty deer hunting rifle and blow my head off. I yearned for death. I craved to be reunited with my mother.

The same day that all of this was about to take place, I got a letter from Ahmad saying that they were shipping him to my prison after he got out of the hole for stabbing up a Gangster Discipline. He said that he would be where I was in a few weeks, and that when he got here, he would have something special for me. I was elated. Finally, I would have some sort of family close. I couldn't wait. The thought of him coming was the only thing that stopped me from following through with my plans to end my life by gun fire.

※

Ahmad showed up a month later. We met in the hole, and they made the mistake of putting us right across the gallery from each other. Every night, we fished kites back and forth with plots of how we were going to take over the drug flow of the prison. Because I had been there for five years already, I knew the ins and outs of the institution. He had a Native chicken that would be down with bringing in the heroin. The only catch was, he couldn't touch the dope because he was now a Muslim, and within Islam it was forbidden.

I didn't care about any of that. I had been broke for too long. He hooked me up with the Native chick, and two months later, I had the prison rocking and rolling. In three months' time, I went from having no money on my books to having five thousand dollars. All the other prison dope boys had to fall back, unless they were paying dues to us or we had come to some sort of an understanding. I didn't fuck with no her of them, but Ahmad had so many friends because the whole prison acted like they wanted to be Muslim. I always found it real hard to listen to him when it came to giving one of his homies a pass or allowing for them to make money. I was deaf to that shit. The way I saw it, they had to get it how I got it and ain't nobody ever gave me a pass in life, so why should I have given another man one? It was fuck the male race for me, and that included the person I hated the most, myself.

When I reached fifteen thousand dollars on my books, that's when I felt comfortable. I started dressing in foreign things from the streets. Stuff like: Jordans, Gucci, Louis, gold watches, and designer frames. I was carrying around cash. The female officers jumped on my heels right away. I paid them to buss moves; to bring in more dope, phones, clothes or jewelry. Most times, I would hit them just because they were single mothers. I could never watch a mother struggle, even to this day. Life started feeling good. I felt like a lion amongst men. Because I started to have so much money, I started looking outside of the prison to see how I could uplift my family that had forgotten about me. I needed love.

CHAPTER 8
THE REVELATION THAT BROKE ME

The world is a jungle. You either fight and dominate or hide and evaporate.
-Unknown

Though I was thankful that Ahmad was with me inside of the prison, even though we were there together, we did our own thing. He looked too much like Alvin for me, and his view of black women made me want to break his jaw every time he spoke.

In addition to his ill viewpoints of my sistas, he had a sick fetish for young girls along with the raping or molesting of them. Every time we spoke, as all men do about sex, he always switched the conversation to his fantasy of basically screwing kids. That would cause us to get into it. We boxed a lot. He won some bouts. I won a bunch.

Another thing that set is apart besides his whole religion was his views of Alvin. He looked at him as if he were a king, even though he hadn't done anything for either of us since we'd been down. He completely forgave him for how he treated our mother and he even condoned both Alvin and Marie's relationship. My mind was blown, so I started to back away from him more and more, all the way up until the time it was his date to go home.

He'd made me so many promises that I never held him to. "Baby bruh, when I get home you ain't gon' want for shit. I'ma write you weekly and keep the phone on. I'ma find your baby mother and your son. I'ma bring him to see you on a regular basis. Just hold ya head. Sit down and write your first book. I'ma get it published for you so all this time will make sense for you."

As soon as he got out, I didn't hear from him for a whole year. He stopped the heroin plug from coming to bless me. He didn't send me any money, and all lines of communication were blocked off unless I bussed a move to open them back up. He never spoke about helping me in any way. Instead, he sent me pictures of him enjoying life to the fullest.

Meanwhile, the women in our family continued to struggle. They were getting evicted left and right. Their cars were getting repossessed, and the children were going hungry. I knocked a forty-year-old, dark-skinned Correctional Officer at the prison and laced her with the game, along with what I was trying to accomplish. She made it very clear that she didn't mind the risk, but for her to go into action, I would have to dick her ass down because she was going through a divorce and needed me to help her forget about it. She said that I needed to bust a move to get to the isolation part of segregation where she was on post for the next thirty days. She was assigned to work this one specific wing on second and third shift. She said once I got down there, she would make sure I got into the room I needed to be in.

As soon as our conversation was over, I walked right up to a loudmouth dude that was known for being a snitch type nigga and I slapped fire from his ass right in front of the officer that he was whispering to. He took off running and I got up against the wall where they handcuffed me and took me to the hole. Sure enough, my female C.O. escorted me to where I needed to be, and that night, I was eleven inches deep in her pussy with a rubber on.

My stipulation was that I refused to fuck her without a rubber, and she was cool with that. During that thirty days, she had me doing some of the freakiest shit to her that I could have never imagined. I enjoyed every single day of it to be honest. After the third week, every time I screwed her, and we fucked every day off and on for forty minutes at a time. She would do her round, and slip back into my room talking that shit, and I would tear her ass up. It didn't start to bother me until she started saying that she loved me, and that she needed to hear me saying that back to her. I had never been one to play about those three words, I couldn't fake it, and I never could tell her that, and that caused her to feel a way. I just upped my sex game and cuddled her more instead of straight fucking. During the thirty days, she bought me four ounces of heroin. I made twenty-five thousand dollars and blessed my whole family, solely the females. I didn't give a fuck about the dudes. I got all of them right. The following month, I did it all again and again the next month, and on and on.

The chocolate officer kept me laced, and all her bills stayed paid. We became emotional but I never fell in love. The only person I was in love with was my mother. I connected love to her. I knew that people could never love or care for you unless you did for them. If you weren't usable in this world then you were worthless. I got it, and I stayed within my own love lane.

About the ninth month that me and the dark-skinned Queen were doing our thing, my little sister Marie sent me a letter that my mother wrote to me on her deathbed. She had one final task for her daughter, and that was to make sure I got this letter after she passed away. The letter was short and sweet. It read:

Dear T.J.

If you are reading this letter it is because your mother has finally passed to what I am hoping will be eternal peace. I am happy to be gone. My life on earth from the day that I was born was oh so painful. I have

A LOVE SO FORBIDDEN THAT ONLY GOD CAN UNDERSTAND

never been loved, cherished, appreciated, catered too, or cared for. My only memories are those of beatings and tragedy. But then there was you... You are the only one that has never lied to me. You have never hurt me, and you have always, I feel, loved me unconditionally. I apologize for all the times that I needed you like Alvin needed Marie, but I am so thankful that you healed me, and that you never crushed my spirits. Though you were my son, you were so much more. You are right now, and forever will be my first true love. If I am to be resurrected, I hope to come back as your other half. It sounds wrong but only you can understand what I mean, Ghost.

I pray that you live a happy life in love, and in Christ. Let me go and know that I am okay. I love you, and you were my everything. Take care sweety, my Taurus. Mama misses you. Always and forever.

P/S Alvin is NOT your biological father, and he knew this. Therefore, he beat you daily. It is a long story that Wendella can explain. Take care my son. Live peacefully.

I read this letter over and over until it began to make sense. It even smelled like her, which drove me crazy. I wrapped it in plastic to preserve its scent and placed it under my pillow. I laid in bed for the next twelve hours, only getting up to use the bathroom, until I found the strength to let it all go. *So, Alvin wasn't my father.* It all made sense. Out of everything that I've ever been given, this news right here was my greatest gift.

CHAPTER 9

MY BROTHER'S KEEPER

Then the LORD said to Cain, "Where is your brother, Abel?"
"I don't know," he replied. "Am I my brother's keeper?"
-Genesis 4:9

"Yeah bruh, I got plenty bad bitches out here. These hoez got hella cash, too. I don't gotta pay for shit. It's a completely different world. You know how it was when you came in back in 2003, and a man had to provide for his woman?"

"Yeah, I remember that. What about it?" I held the phone tighter. The whole conversation with Ahmad had been about him bragging about one thing after the next. Not once had he asked me if I was okay in here.

"Yeah, well, now these hoez pay their way and what they weigh. A man doesn't have to work for shit. It's ten bitchez to every nigga and these hoez know it, especially the black ones." He laughed at that part. "To be honest, niggas don't even fuck wit' black hoez no more. Ma'fuckas trying to get some pretty babies. Not them nappy headed ones that those black bitchez be popping out."

"Dang dawg, don't you know that our mother was black? That should make you feel a way about always shitting on our race of women. Besides, ain't you Muslim?"

"Fuck that got to do with anything, Muslims are all races, but the original culture is Arab and those sistas are yellow and fine as heaven. I been breaking they ass off. A Muslim can have up to four wives; seven depending on which sector you follow. But I did fuck up though."

I was sitting on my prison bed counting fifteen hundred dollars in cash. I needed to hit this new Mexican Correctional Officer that I had knocked to buss moves. She said she needed a gee to do what she needed to do and five hundred for pay. That was light work. "What you mean you messed up?"

"I think I got this black bitch pregnant. At least that's what she talking about. I hope not 'cause she ain't got shit. I just bumped this new bitch with plenty cash, and she looks just like India Arie. She got a good head game, the pussy fire, and she got her own money. That's the main thing. If any black bitch should be pregnant, it should be her."

I shook my head and tucked the money into my underwear. "So, what if shorty is pregnant? Whatchu gon' do then?" I wanted to know. I saw so much of Alvin in Ahmad that it was ridiculous. I prayed that I never became what he and his father was.

"If she is, then I'm screwed. That bitch is a head case. I ain't about to trick off what I got going on to settle down with no bum ass bitch. The pussy good and all of that and she's clingy. I know I got her locked down, but she does too much. Fuck that settling down shit. If I'ma fuck wit' a black bitch, it's gone be this new bitch 'cause she got ends. Even then, I ain't settling down."

"But if there is a kid involved you ain't gon' have no other choice. You gotta be stand up. You gotta be a man. Fuck all of those games, Ahmad." I placed my mirror out of my cell to see down the gallery, then whistled for the Mexican broad to come and get her cash. She came and opened my cell, kissing all over my neck and shit until I pushed her ass out of the room. It wasn't safe.

"Later for that shit you talking, T.J. You just saying that shit because you are in there. Once you are out here, you are going to see how the game goes. I bet you'll side with me. Until then, I'ma keep doing me. If this bitch pregnant, she on her own. I'ma just do for my kid and keep knocking her ass down." He laughed. "She ain't got a pot to piss in though. A bitch gotta be doing something to fuck with me, plus she looks too young to be walking beside me. I don't like those crazy looks."

"Bruh, what made you holler at her in the first place then? Something had to draw you to her." I was getting irritated because here I was trying my best to find my son and his mother. I yearned for my child, and he didn't even want the family that was being afforded to him.

"What made me come at her is because she looked so young, like jailbait. Even when I be fucking, I be imagining she younger than she really is. Mmm. Damn, she got a nice shot on her, though. Her pussy outstanding, and she makes hella noise. Her shit super tight, too, just like a little girl. I'ma send you some pictures."

"Yo', on my mom's, yousa sick ass nigga. Live yo' life though, kid. I wish you the best. You ever run into my baby mother yet?"

"Yeah, she ain't fuckin' wit' you. She said you got too much time. She did get that five gees you sent to her mother for your son, though. She appreciated that and gave me head. Ain't that sumthin'?" He busted up laughing again. "I fucked a few times, too. Her shit straight but not good as the bitch that might be having my kid. It's all good though. I'm a send you some pics of yo' seed, too. Lil' homie is pretty chill."

Did this fuck nigga just say that my bm sucked him up, and he fucked her? Was I tripping? Most of all, why didn't it phase me? "Yo, that's what's good. Anyway, if you see my seed, tell him I love him, and anything he needs, I got him. Find a place I can send him a few more gees to so I can hit him."

"Just send that to me. I'll make sure he gets it. By Allah, I will."

❧

A week later, I sent out twenty-five hundred in cash through the mail. Ahmad received every penny. He told me that he did on the phone and swore he would spend every cent on my child. Later, I found out he did not. He gave my son a hundred-dollar bill, told him that it was from me, then kept the rest and paid his own bills, after taking my son's mother to dinner, followed by a cheap motel. All of this was revealed to me by her years later.

True to his words for the first time, Ahmad did send me pictures of my son and of his child's mother-to-be. But he didn't send me any normal pictures of her. He sent me all lingerie shots of her and three other Spanish females. To say that I didn't study the pictures closely would have been a lie. I surveyed them.

When it came time to throw them away, I tossed the Spanish females in the garbage and kept the pictures of Jelissa Shante. She was super gorgeous. I don't know why I couldn't stop looking at her pictures. It would be these same pictures that I would wind up sending back to her a year or so later, to prove to her that I had them. But for some reason, when I looked over her pictures, I grew a certain longing for her that was not sexual. It wouldn't make sense to me until years later as to why I felt the way I did.

CHAPTER 10
JELISSA

"A strong woman is one who is able to smile this morning like she wasn't crying last night."

Dear Bro,
    I don't wanna take up too much of your time, but I just had to let you know what it was before you allowed for your brother to taint the image you have of me. Today was completely chaotic. Ahmad showed up at my doorstep unannounced, on a weekend he is not supposed to have A'Jhani, telling me that I needed to get our child dressed because he was going to bring him up to the prison to see you. Please keep in mind, he had an enormous opportunity to tell me this yesterday, but he never mentioned it one time. So, when he showed up spur of the moment just like he has done so many times before, I wasn't having it. Besides, I am tired of him playing house with my child. If you are going to see A'Jhani for the first time, I feel like I should be there also. Please understand. I don't have anything against you. Send me a visiting form and I will be there. Happy Birthday by the way.
    Your lil' sis,
    Jelissa

A LOVE SO FORBIDDEN THAT ONLY GOD CAN UNDERSTAND

. . .

I read the letter repeatedly and flipped the envelope over to see if she had left a return address, when I saw that she had I sat down, and got to writing right away. My first letter was short and sweet as well. It read:

Dear Jelissa

First all of all, thank you for reaching out to me to tell me your side of things, especially when you didn't have to. What's fair is fair. If it's not his time to have A'Jhani and he didn't ask you first before he attempted to bring him to me, then you did what you had to do. I don't hold it against you. Stand your ground, and don't allow for yourself to be pushed around or bullied. You are a queen, and you must stand ten toes firm on that reality. I would love to meet you in person, as well as A'Jhani, but all in your good time. However, if there is anything else that you need in the meantime, please let me know, and I will make sure you have it. I appreciate you. Please kiss my nephew for me. Take care lil' Sis.

Your Bro,

T.J.

P.S. Whatever happened to those pictures you promised me a few years back??? Life happens, huh? I get it.

Later Love

It didn't take her but a few days to get back to me. And honestly, I was shocked by her timely response. When they called me up front to receive my mail and I saw her name on the envelope, I found myself feeling a little breathless. I was almost certain that this would be the letter where she told me that she didn't feel right about us corresponding back and forth. I knew how my brother was. He was a major control freak, and even though he made it seem as if he didn't care about her, I knew that within his mind everything was about possession.

I sauntered back to my room and sat on the bed. I took a second to gather myself. I could smell the perfume coming from her letter, and for some reason that made me smile. *Damn, she had to know that I would catch a whiff of that scent. I wonder if she did that on purpose?* I shook the thought out of my head. This was my brother's baby mother. I was sure that she wasn't thinking along those lines of attraction. I wasn't supposed to have been either. Right?

Her letter began as the other one had:

Dear Bro,

I hope this letter finds you blessed and in the best of health. Since I wrote to you last week, things have gotten just a bit crazier. Your brother has started to call me out of my name a lot. He insists that I don't have to make any more friends, even though he can parade around town as an engaged man.

He pops up at my house at all hours of the day and night, and more than once, he has run my company away. He has developed a habit of forcing himself upon me, and as you know, I am way too weak to fight him off. He does the bare minimum for A'Jhani, but then he promotes himself as the best father in the world. He talks to me as if I'm an idiot; like my thoughts, feelings, and emotions don't matter. He shows a lack of interest within Rae'Jon now that he is with this new female. I don't know. I just feel so low. So trapped. This is my second child, by a second man. I am in no position to lose him.

There are already so many people that are ashamed and disappointed in me. So many held high hopes for me. I never wanted to be a statistic. I was supposed to be the girl that became something great. I feel so alone, and like a prisoner in my circumstances. I wish I could have a redo. I mean, I love my children. I am thankful that they are here, healthy, beautiful and strong, but I just wish they could have come at a later date. Within better circumstances and with my husband. Not two individuals that I feel were mistakes.

I am sorry for rambling on. I hope you don't tell your brother any of these things. I fear what he would do to me. He threatens me a lot, and he has such a standing within the community that he can paint me out to be anything that he wants, and they would believe him. In addition to the community support, he also has the Temple behind him. Those Blackstone

A LOVE SO FORBIDDEN THAT ONLY GOD CAN UNDERSTAND

dudes. I've seen enough to let me know that whenever he wants me six feet under it will happen. I hate my life right now. I can't stop crying as I write this. Life is so unfair. So one sided. All I've ever wanted was to be loved by a man. By my father, and that love was never received. I am broken. Damaged goods.

I pray I didn't dampen your day my brother. Thank you for listening. Writing to you has been so therapeutic for me. I'm pretty sure it only causes you irritation and stress. Lol. I apologize, but this is just where I am right now. Moreover, I have lost touch with my mother. I think her disappointment within me is outweighing the love right now. The story of my life.

Before I forget, I will be sending those much-needed pictures tomorrow. God bless you bro.

Your sis,
Jelissa

I must have reread this letter over and over for like twenty minutes. I couldn't help shaking my head and cursing under my breath. Her story seemed mildly reminiscent of my mother's. I could tell that Ahmad was going to slowly turn into our father over time. There seemed to be so much going on that it had my mind wandering like crazy. The one thing amongst many that stood out to me was how well written, and neat her letter was. Alongside that was the mention of Ahmad forcing himself on to her. That made me so angry and so heated that I felt like exploding. How could any man force himself upon a woman? How could a man have a child by a woman, leave her to marry another, then run in and out of the child's mother's life just to cause her pain and discord? I didn't get it.

Along with all these things, I couldn't help but to tune into the part of her letter where she said that all she wanted to be was loved. That had been me my entire life. All I've ever wanted to be was loved by *one* person. I never needed a bunch. Just one person that loved me unconditionally. I would go oh so hard for that person with everything that I stood for as a man. I just down right didn't think that I was eligible for that kind of love, so I stopped believing that it existed. Instead of going on about my day, I sat at my desk and wrote Jelissa a twenty-three-page letter, but I will keep it short and sweet here. The gist of it said this...

Dear Jelissa,

First and foremost, I apologize on behalf of my brother for all the things that he is taking you through, and for all the ways he has hurt you. Real men don't behave in that fashion. When a man truly loves a woman, every time she hurts, he will hurt as well. There is no such thing as a man loving you or even caring about you for that matter, if he can impregnate you, and then leave you for another woman who has not borne his seed. His place should always be beside you. Only a coward will impregnate a woman and then leave her to fend for herself, or until he needs her sexually. That's selfish. It's immature and it's disgusting. I am so, so sorry. Please do not stop to think for one second that his actions reflect my character, or that all men are like that, even if it has been your experience with the male population thus far.

Beautiful sister, you must find your voice. You must find your inner peace, but most importantly you must find the love for yourself first. You must love yourself first. This is a task that even I struggle with. I hate myself because of where I come from and the things that I've been through. I have, like you, never been loved before. I have never been cared about or anything of the sort. My entire life has been nothing but heartache and pain. But this letter isn't about me. I need for you to know that you are mighty. You are great. You are a woman. You have given life, not once but twice. Those are things that no man could ever do. As a woman, you are stronger than a man. You can endure more. You are more patient. More cerebral. You have the ability to flip the script, and to overpower and consider any man by just using what God has given you which is your womanhood.

I do not condone anything that Ahmad has done thus far. That shit is weak to me. I love him, but what's right is right. Because of their being a child involved, and me knowing the circumstances of how my brother is,

I have to side with what is right in honor of my mother. With that being said I am with you one hundred percent. I know you barely know me, and I never use these three words, but I love you, and I got you. I am here for you. Anything that you need please let me know. I will fill in the blanks for you. Test me. That's all I ask. Test me.

I don't want to make this letter longer than it has to be. It's already ten plus pages. I just needed you to know that I am siding with you one hundred percent. Real men can NOT be loyal to bullshit. I am loyal to this truth, and what's deep inside of me.

I love you, Jelissa. Kiss my nephews for me.

Your bro.

I sat there on the bed wondering if I was really going to have enough nerve to send it out. I know that once this letter was mailed that I had chosen a side. I thought about all the things that Jelissa had written to me about. I imagined them vividly and compared them to what I remembered going through as a child and what I'd witnessed. My eyes got watery. I got up, placed the letter inside of the envelope, and sealed it before mailing it out. I came back and worked my body out like crazy thinking about Jelissa and the lines I had just crossed. I only felt guilty for a moment. Then I shook off the feeling and smiled because of the thoughts that were going through my head.

CHAPTER 11
LOVE AND WAR

"All's fair in love and war."
-Francis Edward Smedley

"Bruh, I know that bitch been writing you for a lil' minute now. I don't want you fuckin' wit' her no more. She got me locked the fuck up, and I didn't even do shit. I knew I shouldn't have been fuckin' wit that ratchet ass, broke bitch." Ahmad snapped, as he sat across the table from me on one of the few visiting times that he'd actually come out to see me.

Alongside of him was Brenda; a dark-skinned, India Arie look alike that Ahmad swore up and down was perfect to be his wife. What he didn't know was that directly after he'd gotten arrested for physically assaulting Jelissa and trying to kidnap A'Jhani, this Brenda broad had made it her business to drive up to see me on multiple occasions, and she made it perfectly clear that she was trying to get smashed, sexed, fucked, dicked down, you get the drift. I never did it because that wasn't me. There was no attraction there for me, and mentally I was already invested within Jelissa as crazy as that sounded.

"Yo, kid, so you telling me that you didn't beat her up at grandma's crib on the fourth of July last year? She made all of that shit up?" I took a swallow from my Sprite pop and glanced over at his wife-to-be who winked at me. I ignored her.

"Hell yeah, I whooped her ass. That bitch deserved it. She ain't got no right trying to break-up me and my wife. All that lil' shit I was telling her was necessary, so she didn't ever get on any bullshit with me seeing my son. Fuck I look like? I don't give a fuck about her."

By this time, Jelissa and I had been writing and talking on the phone for about eight months. I felt a way about her, and I wasn't feeling how bro kept calling her out of her name and degrading her. I felt like he was Alvin, and he was speaking about my defenseless mother all over again. I was sweating because I was so heated.

"But yeah, I got something for that bitch though. Don't nobody cross me and get away with it." He nodded his head and cracked his knuckles. He looked over to Brenda and smiled. "We got that bitch don't we baby?" Brenda nodded her head and sipped from her bottle of water.

I couldn't take it anymore. I was a Taurus after all. "Fuck you got for her?" I mugged him. "You talking like y'all got some fuck shit up y'all sleeves. Don't you understand that this is your son's mother? So what the fuck y'all got going on?"

Brenda pushed her seat back from the table and crossed her legs. "Damn, why you getting all defensive over her? Y'all done got that close in a few months?" She was jealous, and it was obvious.

"Yo, be quiet, I'm talking to dis nigga." I snapped. "What you got up your sleeve, Ahmad? Tell me? "

He smiled wickedly. "Alexa n'em' just moved up here from Chicago. I'm finna have her and a couple of her friends beat the shit out of her. Then if she still on bullshit, Tracy gon' get rid of her the real way. You know, on that Edwards' family type shit."

Now my fingers were balled into fists. "That nigga Tracy

shiesty ass here, now?" Tracy was our cousin. He was known for being a rapist, murderer, and a hired hit man. If bro called him up front Chicago that meant that he had plans on killing Jelissa. I was vexed.

"I gave him five gees as soon as I got out and told him to stand by. That nigga ready to move right now. I'ma wait until I get my son this weekend and have him take care of that bidness, fuck the ass whooping now that I think about it. Yeah, I want this bitch gone. "

"Oh yeah." Now I was fidgeting in my seat. "Yeah well I guess you gotta do what you gotta do then. And you sure you gon' have, Tracy handle dis bidness when you get yo seed from her this next time? "

"Yeah, by Allah she gotta go. All you gotta do is keep doing what you doing. Don't say shit. This bitch ain't even gon' know what's coming." He rubbed his hands together and laughed sadistically.

I scooted back just a bit. I needed to create a little space between myself, and both of them. The visiting room was already small. The table seemed as if it were meant for a kindergarten class. I could smell his cologne, and Brenda's perfume. It was enough to make me sick on the stomach. "Bruh, I gotta just say this. That is your child's mother. If you whack her then your seed ain't gon' have a mother. Do you know how that is going to affect him growing up, especially if his mother is murdered?"

"I'll be his mother." Brenda cut in. "A'Jhani is a beautiful baby. He seems like he loves me way more than he does her anyway. That's probably why she is so jealous."

"Yeah bruh, my wife is all the mother that my son's gon' need. He'll be alright. Plus, he so young that it's more than likely that he won't even remember her ass anyway. Either way I am willing to roll the dice. Tracy already paid, and he is sleeping on grandma's couch. She don't want that nigga being there for too long because you already know his past."

"Times up, Edwards." The guard came to the table to tell me this. I was happy to hear those words. I stood up, and reluctantly hugged Ahmad. "Yo, be careful out there bruh. Hold ya head, and I'll see you soon." I broke the embrace, and Brenda nearly snapped her neck to get to me. I hugged her and tried to release her. She held me tighter for a few seconds before she let me go.

"Alright baby brother, I'll bring A'Jhani to see you next week, Allah willing. Until then staying yo' Qur'an. Allah will bless those that seek him. Assalamualaikum. .

When I got back to the unit I went into overdrive. I got straight on the phone and called in a few favors from a trusted Latin King homie from back in Chicago that I went to school with. Since I'd been in the joint he had become my heroin connection. He picked up on the first ring, and we talked serious business for the next hour. I dropped him ten gees flat, and the conversation ended. (Side note, there is no statute of limitations for certain crimes, so I gotta keep this section brief.)

However, that night, I sent Jelissa Shane eight five hundred dollars and told her to go to a hotel for a few days. I told her there would be more to come, but for now she needed to leave Madison. I told her that she was in some serious danger and that she needed to not ask a bunch of questions, just to trust me, and no matter what happens do not give A'Jhani to Ahmad. That she needed to stall for a few days. Though she was scared out of her mind she listened to me, and I am so thankful that she did because had she not I am almost sure that things would have gone south very swiftly.

Two days after she packed up and moved into a hotel three hours away from Madison where she previously resided, our cousin Tracy was shot fifteen times coming out of a gas station by my grandmother's home. He died on the scene, and his killers were never found. At the revelation of his death the feds went on live television and spoke about how they had been looking for him for three years. He was supposed to have been responsible for over fifteen rapes, and ten murders of women. I could tell from the news conference that the authorities felt a sigh of relief. This only angered me because I knew that had everything gone Ahmad's way, Jelissa would have been the next casualty for Tracy. What type of man would do such a thing to his children's mother? I didn't get it.

Ahmad showed up to the prison the following week with Brenda in tow. He was heated, and full of fire when I walked through the door. We didn't hug, I sat down. He remained standing. "Bitch ass nigga, it was you wasn't it? "

"Yo, where the fuck is the food for me to eat, Ahmad? You know how dis shit go, whenever you come to see me you gotta have something on the table for me to eat. Yo, Brenda, go snatch me up some snacks." She jumped up to follow my commands, shaking her as that didn't impress me one bit. As soon as she was out of ear shot I stood up. "Nigga, you ain't nothing but a new version of Alvin. I couldn't stop him from killing my mother, or hurting her, but this is my second chance. I'm taking Jelissa. This me now. Take that shit how you want too." What was crazy was that I hadn't even gotten the okay from Jelissa that we were going to be together, but deep in my heart I just knew.

He turned a bright shade of reddish brown. "So you kill a nigga from our bloodline for this bitch? Really, you don't even know her. On top of that you dare to cross me? Really, have you lost your mind?"

"Nigga I ain't do shit, I'm in prison. You sound like the police with all of these speculations. Secondly, fuck Tracy rapist ass. That bitch nigga only targeted women, he got what he deserved. Thirdly, I ain't cross you, I'm doing what's best for her, and me. Fuck you. You already know how I am. I said what I said. The line has been drawn in the sand. Keep that drama shit to yourself and be a father to your child. If you try and hurt Jelissa nigga we gon' have some serious issues. That's me now. You plot on or hurt her in any way from here on out it is equivalent to you doing it to me. That's what it is."

Brenda came back with the food and set it before me. She leaned all the way over to make sure that I got a good look down here braless shirt. "Okay Ghost, this should make you happy." She stood back and looked up at me. "You good?"

"This bitch ass nigga fuckin' wit' Jelissa on some other shit. He stopped Tracy from killing her ass. Now, he acting like he's ready to go to war over her. " Ahmad spat. He took his glasses off and sat them on the table.

Brenda stepped back, caught off guard. "Her skinny ass! What the fuck is so good about her that y'all desire this bitch so much? I don't get it." She crossed her arms.

"Watch yo' mouth, shorty. And nigga you watch yo mouth, too. Y'all got each other, that should make the both of you happy. All he gotta do is keep that four shit to himself and be a father. He ain't gotta worry about shit that me and her got going on. That ain't his bidness."

"My bidness, oh yeah nigga?!" He hopped over the table and tried to jump on top of me. I side stepped him and punched him three quick times in the jaw knocking him to the floor. He hopped up and rushed me swearing up and down that he was going to kill me.

Brenda screamed for us to stop. I held up my guards and swung four haymakers after he bust my lip. The hits dropped him to his knees. The guards rushed me and tackled me to the floor. Ahmad jumped up and stomped me in the back of the head twice, got to his knees and punched me five times in the face busting my nose, mouth, and eye.

I struggled to get up. The guards kept me pinned. He and Brenda ran out of the visiting room. I was drug to the hole, bloody and battered. I wound up getting seven months in the hole for that and was transferred back to the prison of Waupun and my custody was elevated once again to maximum security status, once I got to Waupun the war proceeded to get even more real between he and I, and there was a lot of bloodshed that followed this event.

CHAPTER 12
A COVENANT IN BLOOD

Greater love has no one than this: to lay down one's life for one's friends.
-John 15:13

When I got back to Waupun I had to go into overdrive on the huddling tip because at my request, Jelissa had moved hours away from her the city where she he been living, and I promised her that if she did that I would do everything that I could to make sure I met her more than half way with all of the bills. I didn't know how I was going to live up to that promise, but I knew that I would.

What was bananas about this whole thing was the fact that I hadn't even met her in person yet. We had a talent for writing to each other, longer, in depth letters. Mine averaged twenty pages, and her's, closer to ten. We talked on the phone for eight hours daily and did everything that we could to stay in tune with each other, short of visits.

I don't know how it was that I found myself falling more and more in love with her when I had not even seen her in person, but I did. Jelissa's words spoke to my soul. Her heart seemed so pure. Her voice was like that of the ocean crashing into the shore. Her laugh like the greatest song ever sang. Her letters made me feel special, whole, and loved. I became obsessed with the emotional parts of her, and the fact that she could bring that side out of me by just asking questions and listening said a lot.

She was always so concerned, so worried, so thankful for me. She prayed for me. She sent me her last even when I never asked for it. Her homemade cards made me feel like she sat down, took her time and crafted something special just for me. Her time and presence was so important to me that I started to fear losing it. Even though I didn't know if God was listening or not, every night I got down on my knees, and I prayed up to Him, begging Him to just allow for me to have Jelissa as my wife. I had promised to stop doing so many negative things if I could have her. I didn't want fortune or fame. All I wanted was her and the unconditional love that she had for me.

I'd seen an interview with a certain celebrity and she was saying that before all of her dreams came to pass she wrote them down in her Bible and prayed about them every day. She said that slowly but surely they started to come, just one after the other. That piqued my interest.

The next day I did just that. I sat down, and the first thing I wrote in my Bible was that I wanted for God to make Jelissa my wife, and I prayed to Him about it. "Father, I know that I am a sinner, and I don't deserve unconditional love, but I come to You humbly, and submissive. I am begging for you to grant me this one precious gift that I know that I am it worthy of. Father, please make Jelissa Shantè my wife. Please Lord. If you could grant me this I promise to convert solely to Christianity. I promise to do all that I can to become a kingdom man. I promised to love and cherish her. I promise to never cheat, or to purposely hurt her. I promise to love, honor, and protect her. I promise to embrace and love her children as my own. I promise to provide for them, if you can show me how. Father, you know that I am a dope boy. I love to hustle, and to get money the wrong way. Show me another way. Help me to change into the man that You need for me to be for her. Help me to be everything that she needs and desires. In Jesus' holy and precious name I pray, Amen."

I don't know where the tears came from, or when they started but my face was drenched, and so was my shirt. I stood up light headed and lost. I took a moment to gather myself before I washed my face and stepped out into the dark castle of Waupun on my grind to make sure that I could pay the rent for the up and coming month.

In a weeks' time, I was back in action. I sold heroin, pills, weed, and even sex magazines. I didn't want any canteen. Anything I sold, the buyer had to have his family on the street send the funds directly into an account I had set up out there. Jelissa never touched it until the end of the month. It was my job to make sure that at the end of the month, there was always enough to cover the rent, car note, all insurances, cable bill, and phone bills.

I felt that was the least I could do even though she told me that she had it, and I didn't have to. I insisted, because in my mind that is what being a man is all about. The stigma that a man being in prison meant that he can't help out with the bills, or that he can't get his own money was bullshit. Most of the dudes in prison were just lazy, and they're priorities were out of whack. If a man really loved his family, he would always find a way to provide for them. That's what real men do. Anything contrary to him making it happen for you or his children was an excuse.

Leave his ass, bums should never be invested in. They are a pure waste of time. Sistas know your worth.

"Yo, Ghost, I got something crazy to tell you, and I don't want you to snap out because there are only four of us that know this is about to go down." Ready Rock, a heroin junky said to me four hours before my side of the building was scheduled to go to rec.

I was already in my cell doing push-ups. I stood up glistening in sweat. "What's good bruh? Why you look all spooked and shit?" I walked closer to the bars. They were locked. Ready Rock was assigned as a tier runner by the prison. He was in charge of passing the phones back and forth between cells and handing out the meal trays. Because his job afforded him so much privilege he always got the information around the prison fresh off the presses. He also kept tabs on the police for me. He was super tighter with them which was important. Because of him I avoided raids, and a bunch of losses

"Say Ghost, I got some fire information baby, you gon' wanna look out for me real nice." He scratched his inner forearm and danced from one foot to the next. He was fifty plus, dark-skinned, bald headed, skinny with only a few teeth.

"Spill the beans, nigga. You already know that if it's worth it I'll bless you." I was already well ahead of my quota on the bills. I had a little something extra I could lace him with if it came down to it.

"Alrighty man, damn, I'm just gon' spit it out. They got yo' hit plotted out for tonight. These fools are about to kill you in the showers up at rec. They got the police on the payroll, man yousa' dead man. What you gon' do baby?" He scratched the back of his neck and looked from left to right.

"How many, and who is calling for my hit?" I wasn't afraid. I had started to take prayer more seriously. I had been asking God to make me a sacrifice. To place me within a situation where I could prove how much I loved and wanted Jelissa. I begged for him to help me enter into a covenant with the two of them.

"It's three of them. They got three-inch blades that I just passed to them from the Muslims. They said that your own brother is calling for your hit. He said you raped his daughters and he just found out. I know that shit ain't true, is it?"

"My brother ain't got no fuckin' daughters. He ain't got but one son. This dude is petty. How much bread he put up?" I needed to know what type of hit I was dealing with. The more money a person put up in prison determined what kind of killers they were hiring. Over five thousand and they were coming to kill you. Less than that and they were more than likely coming to maim you. Ahmad hadn't been paying his child support at this time, and he was always claiming that the reason why was because he was broke. I already knew that he couldn't have any paper to pay for a serious move.

"He put up ten thousand dollars and got one of the dudes, a lawyer. This is serious. What are you going to do?" Ready Rock started scratching himself again.

I went into my stash and gave a sixteenth of heroin. It was worth six hundred in Waupun. "Yo, keep yo' mouth shut, and let me handle this. You ain't told me shit. I'll holler bruh."

Ready Rock licked his lips. "I don't know what you got planned but be careful. I love you, Ghost. You good nigga. Yo' own brother though, damn. " He walked away from the cell.

I laid on my bed for a moment. "Damn, so this is the sacrifice right here huh, Lord?" I smiled, "my mama always said that You had a sense of humor. " I took a deep breath. Well then, here goes nothing."

❦

Before I went to rec that night I called Jelissa Shantè. She picked up on the third ring. "Hey king, how are you doing?" I could hear the sounds of Jhenè Aiko in the background. My stomach turned over a few times before I was able to speak. She must have sensed this. "What's the matter?"

"So...," I paused for a second. I wanted to tell her what he was about to go down, but for some reason I couldn't bring myself to do so. I felt like I was about to head out to my death, and the only thing that I wanted for this woman to know was how much I loved and cared about her amongst a few other things.

"T.J., you are scaring me. What's the matter?" The music cut off on the other end. The phone sounded like it was being clicked off speakerphone. "Hello?"

"So, I've been reading the Bible a lot lately, you know, because of you and everything. And one of the things I am struggling to understand is the concept of covenants." I started to shake as I looked at the alarm clock that was set directly next to my bed. It told me that there was fifteen minutes left before rec. I started to shake.

"Okay, so what are you trying to figure out?"

Once again I was quiet. I knew how they got down with knives and shanks in Waupun. Most of the dudes that were here were placed here because they were serious killers. This was the prison that they sent you to when you were too dangerous to be anywhere else. I was more than sure that for ten thousand dollars, these dudes were about to kill me. I sighed as my heart began to beat faster.

"Jelissa, I need for you to know that I love you. There is nothing in this world that I would not render unto you, and there is nothing, no obstacle that I would refuse to overcome for you. I want to enter into this covenant with you. I wanna be with you for the rest of my life. I wanna sacrifice myself for you by any means."

"I know you do, baby, but we have to continue to seek first the kingdom of God and then all of His righteousness will be added unto us. We have so far to go, and so much to learn before we enter into a territory where it is all or nothing. God knows when the time is right."

"Yo, I feel you, but I may not get that much time baby. I need you to know that I love you right now, and that I am willing to die for you. I know that there have been so many losers that you have crossed paths with. I am not one of them. I am all about you, and all about those babies. But a man's words mean nothing unless actions accompany them. So, I'ma show you what I mean, and who I am. When I do, and the good Lord blesses me to keep life within my body, you gotta be my wife. You have to marry me, and we need to do this day for day. We have to build a whole foundation together that will be unbreakable. Promise me this."

"Baby, I am here for you. But drastic steps like that takes time. We have so much to build, and so many obstacles to climb before we slam our feet on the gas. There are the children to think about. The broken relationships with our families and so many other things. We need to ensure that this is what we really want, and that we can really handle it. You are his brother. You are A'Jhani's uncle. Down the line, are we really willing to take what all comes with that?"

"No covenant can be sealed without the shedding of blood. I declare right now before Jehovah and Jesus Christ that you will be my wife. I am willing to shed blood for you to secure this covenant. If Jehovah allows for me to live after whatever takes place, it is meant for you to be my wife. If I die, then it was never meant to be. It is what it is. I love you, and you are my One. Jehovah will prove this. Later, baby." I hung up the phone and hopped off of my bed.

Ready Rock stood at the cage. "Say Ghost, I gotta ask you man, they told me to come and ask you should I say. Are you willing to drop ol' girl and come back to the brothers, or are you willing to receive whatever is coming to you for going against the grain?"

Four of my homies came up beside Ready Rock with their gym clothes. They gave me the look that said, *bruh, we with you. We will send this bitch up if anybody thinks they gon' touch you.* I was feeding all of them and their families. I knew they would rather die in battle than to allow for anybody to do anything to me.

"Yo Ready Rock, tell whoever sent you I said to go fuck they self. Tell 'em that's my Queen, and I ain't duckin' no action." My heart pounded in my chest.

Ready Rock nodded. "Damn Ghost, she's worth all of that!" He shook his head, "awright man." He walked away from the cage.

As soon as he left, I turned to my homies. "Bruh, ain't none of you niggas going to rec tonight. Y'all gon' chill on the gallery and miss this one." They argued me up and down about why I was tripping and how I was making a huge mistake. That they knew that tonight was the night I was supposed to be killed, and that if they weren't there to prevent it, I would be. But no matter what they said or how they tried to spin it, my mind was made up. I was ready to die.

CHAPTER 13
PAIN IS LOVE

"You can sacrifice and not love. But you cannot love and not sacrifice."
-Kris Vollotton

It was six twenty-five in the evening. The gymnasium was packed more than usual this day. The basketball court was crowded with a bunch of prisoners doing their best to live out their hoop dreams. They hooped and hollered from the sidelines, while others stretched their limbs to get prepared to get the court next. It didn't matter where I walked that night, it seemed that all eyes water on me. I felt like I was the new kid at a new school, and my parents had dressed me in nothing but bright clothing. More than a few dues had walked past me and whispered, "Yo, Ghost, don't shower tonight homie, the word is that they gon' kill you in there." Then they would saunter off quickly.

You see, even though I was a savage and I held my own, I had never been one to take advantage of anybody. I kept my word, I was respectful, and I always did for those that were less fortunate than myself. I just didn't take no bullshit from nobody, but many loved and respected me. In this cold hearted prison that was supposed to be the roughest in the state, I saw so many compassionate faces of men that felt sorry for me because they were sure that this night was the night that I was going to die. It was humbling.

Instead of heeding the warnings, I took deep breath and headed toward the showers where a few gang bangers had them closed off. They were only allowing for certain individuals to use them. As I approached the showers, the police officer who was assigned to that post, avoided eye contact with me. As he got up and walked past me, he folded his newspaper under his arm and began to whistle. I already knew what that meant. He meant that he had been paid off to turn the other cheek. The system was so corrupt. As long as you could pay your way, you could control anything.

When I got to the showers, the gang bangers that were holding down the entrance moved to the side, after nodding their head at me. I ignored them and stepped inside. It felt like the entire world flipped dark for a moment and everything moved in slow motion.

The door slammed behind me just as two dudes jumped from the bathroom stalls. Another stepped out of the showers. All three had blades in their hands and two of the three looked afraid to perform the task that was at hand. They surrounded me. The leader, a dark skinned, triple lifer, spoke up. "Dis yo' hit my nigga. Any last words?" He spit on the floor right next to my feet.

I thought about Jelissa and took a deep breath. "No weapons formed against me shall prosper. I don't fear you niggas, do what you gotta do." I closed my eyes for a second and the triple lifer punched me so hard that I flew into the wall. My face hit the side of it hard. The next thing I knew, I was grabbed around the neck from behind and I felt the blade going into me over and over again.

It felt like the worst bee stings in the entire world again and again. I felt the blood pouring out of me. After a series of stabs, he turned me around and raised his blade with the speed of lightning. He brought it down full speed and tried to slam it into my heart. The blade hit the meat between my left shoulder blade and chest cavity and got stuck. He struggled to get it out for a moment before he and the duo fled the scene, after saying "Ahmad said rest in hell!"

I laid on my side as everything became blurry. Slowly, the color of the world began to turn gray. A puddle formed around my body. My eyes rolled into the back of my head, and I passed out.

Two days later, when I woke up, I was in the hospital with IVs and many things attached to me that made me feel like a robot. I was chained to the bed and a guard, the same guard that had allowed for this to happen to me, was assigned my post. When he saw that I was awake, he smiled.

"What's so funny?" I asked with my throat drier than sand. I was in so much pain that I couldn't think straight.

"I just won a hundred dollars. They were sure that you would die before this afternoon, but look at you, you're going to make it aren't you?" He laughed. "Aw, boy, you prisoners are hilarious."

"Yo, what's good with my phone call? I'm supposed to get one phone call." I wanted to hear Jelissa's voice. I needed to hear her voice. I felt so weak.

"This ain't no goddamn county jail. You belong to the state of Wisconsin which means that you get what we give you, when we give it to your black ass. So shut the fuck up and enjoy those drugs they want to put you on. " He flipped out his newspaper and covered his face.

"Yo', fuck you man. I don't need no drugs. Y'all can't put that bullshit in my system without my consent, that's a lawsuit. I don't want that shit in me."

"Which is why it ain't. You wanna sit there and suffer, then so be it. Hell, if it was me and somebody stabbed me sixteen times, I would be higher than hell. You are one of a kind. How 'bout you get the drugs and give them to me?"

"Yo', kiss my ass man. Leave me alone. I need to be released so I can make my phone call. That's all I wanna do."

"Yeah, well, that ain't happening here. Lay back and suffer. You'll be here for two more days, they say. You gon' eat this pudding?" He grabbed it from my tray and opened it.

I closed my eyes and tried my best to hear Jelissa's voice. I prayed that she would be okay. I knew that somebody had contacted her about my stabbing by now. I didn't want her to suffer in worry. I was okay. Jehovah had allowed for me to live. That meant that He loved me, and that I was supposed to be with Jelissa. That our covenant was sealed by blood. I was so happy. So thankful. I was ready for what came next. All I wanted to do was to hear her voice and to see her.

❦

They released me a week later. Because I refused to tell them the individuals that tried to murder me the prison placed me in the worst part of the institution's hole thinking that it would break me to snitch. They kept me there for nearly a month and then they released me. But before they released me back to population I was able to make one ten minute phone call to Jelissa the same day I was released from the hospital. Here's how it went.

She picked up already in tears. "Baby, are you okay? Please tell me that you are okay?" My gauze was saturated in blood and needed to be changed. I was in so much pain that I had to take a deep breath to keep from passing out. "Yo', I'm good cutie. I can't say much, but I'm good. You know they can't kill what God got protected. "

She cried harder. "Why did this happen? It was all because of me wasn't it? Maybe, we should call things. Maybe your family was right. We can't-"

"Never! There is no covenant without the shedding of blood. I shed blood for you because I love you. You are supposed to be my wife. This was necessary. I am for you, and I am going to be your sacrifice until my last breath. They gon' have to kill me to keep me away from you because you are my Church. I am your Christ. I love you and look forward to time for us to come together in the physical. I got a few more weeks under investigation. Then I'm free. I need you. "

"You have one minute left to talk." Came the institution's phone recording.

"Nooooooo!" Jelissa snapped. "When will I hear from you again?"

"As soon as I get the phone, you will be my only call. I love you. I honor you. I am going to cherish you, and I submit to you. Forevermore."

"I love you, too, bro. Please be safe." The phone clicked dead.

I handed it back out to the guards and collapsed on the floor. My body gave out. I lay there with my eyes wide open, happy, and missing her. Slowly, I drifted out of consciousness as the guards came into the room to rush me back to the hospital.

CHAPTER 14
THE UNION

For this reason a man shall leave his father and mother and be joined to his wife, and the two shall become one flesh'; so then they are no longer two, but one flesh.
-Mark 10:7-8

I had never been more nervous in all of my life to meet nobody, but for some reason I was sweating, and freaking out about meeting Jelissa for the first time in person. I mean one thing that I could say about myself was the fact that I had never been one to settle for a female that didn't physically appeal to me in every single way, so I was accustomed to aligning myself with a beautiful woman but this woman was so much more than beautiful.

Not only was she sexy and appealing to my sexual nature, but her mental capabilities and the higher elevation that she spoke from drew me to her on a whole 'nother level. It was like deep down inside of the fibers of my being I knew that she was my one, and I yearned to connect with her on a physical level that would captivate the spiritual emptiness that I felt deep down within my soul.

They called me at three-forty-one in the afternoon and told me that I had a visitor in the lobby waiting to see me. I started to shake. I stepped inside of the cell's mirror one last time and exhaled loudly. I find every flaw, every blemish within my face that told me that I wasn't god enough to meet such an attractive woman. I was nervous and insecure. I don't know where my confidence had gone. I was Ghost, T.J., and some of the fellas even called me Hood Rich because of my crazy dope boy mentality.

I was accustomed to messing around with gorgeous women of all races, and ever since I had been at the prison only the baddest of the bad women wanted to mess with me, but it wasn't until Jelissa stepped into the picture that I began to turn them down. But I say that to say, I was on top of my game everywhere else, but when it came to Jelissa I was afraid, which was probably why I hadn't pushed for us to meet face to face sooner. I was too insecure.

I ran a cold towel over my face and stood back looking over my reflection. "Yo', it is what it is. I applied my cologne and slipped my glasses over my eyes and headed out. The visiting room was about two city blocks away and sight every step that I took I became more and more nervous.

When I got there, one of the guards I held a financial account with nodded. "Wheew, you got yourself quite the dame out there. You wanna cash in some of that money you got with me? It'll only run you a thousand. There aren't any ass holes working on shift with me. Today is the perfect time."

I didn't even know if Jelissa would go for any sex type shit, but at the very least this was her first time being in a prison so she might have wanted to be alone with me out of the public eye. A thousand dollars was definitely worth that. "Cool, but make sure that ma'fucka clean. Yo', don't have me paying ya' ass if I'm bringing my Queen into some kind of filth. Nah' mean?"

"The only thing I heard was that we are down to fifteen hundred once I make this happen for you. Illegal handle my end. Intact I'll get a janitor in there right now. No refunds. So, if she doesn't wanna go, your money is already cashed in. See you in ten minutes."

"Yeah, whatever. " I shook my head and carried on my way.

When I stepped through the doors of the visiting room I saw that it was packed. There were people from wall to wall. I didn't know how in the hell I was going to find her. I headed up to the desk to give the officers my visiting pass and continued to scan the room. It looked like baby mother central. Kids were running all around, and it was so loud that I couldn't even hear myself think.

As I was coming back from the desk I spotted her. She sat at the table in a pink dress with a slit on the side of it that fell away to reveal a dark caramel thigh that was just the right size for me. Her long braids were full of sheen. They rested across her chest, and down her back. She turned her head sideways and took a bite of a Pop Tart. The crumbs scattered to the table, he ignored them, and kept her eyes wide. Hers locked with mine, and I became nervous. Damn she was fine. I gotta man up.

I headed over to her. The closer I got the more confident, and the more possessive I became, especially because I could see every other dude in the room looking at her as if they wanted to eat her alive. Not to mention my name rang bells throughout the prison so everybody wanted to see and know who I was coming to visit.

As I approached closer, I was now four feet away from her chair and she stared at me with doe eyes. She didn't move, and that was a shot at my ego. I just knew that I didn't measure up. She must have been regretting coming. *Damn, why was this happening to me?*

"You better get yo' lil' fine ass up and give me my kiss." I demanded, sounding more confident than I actually was. She blinked twice and stood up as if she were moving on auto pilot.

She closed the distance in between us. I snatched her up, lifted her into the air and turned her around for a minute. Then I placed her back on the ground and looked into her pretty brown eyes before I kissed her soft, perfect, juicy lips that caused my knees to buckle momentarily.

I felt the stabbings in my back as if they were happening in that moment all over again. Each puncture worth the pain, worth the agony for the kisses that she rendered on to me. We tongued each other down for two whole minutes, until I was fully erect, and that had never happened to me before. I could barely breathe. Her scent, her feel, her warmth, her presence was enough to emit precum from my penis. I groaned into her mouth and felt embarrassed.

I stepped back. "Yo', come with me for a minute, I got something that I wanna show you, and I can't show you out here." She appeared nervous. She looked both ways. "Okay, let me grab my quarters. " She grabbed the bag and followed me to the back. Once there the guard smiled. "I know I promised you an hour, but it has to be forty finger minutes. The window is tight, Illegal owe you fifteen minutes, don't argue with me on this, please. But of course I did, and that cost us five more minutes. Finally I relented, and both myself and Jelissa Shantè wound up in a private room, alone and both just as vulnerable as the other.

She sat on the bed, I could tell that she was nervous. I closed the door and pulled down the shade. "Look Boo." I pulled my shirt over my head and turned away from her so that she could see my injuries. She hopped out of the bed and rushed to me. Her fingers played over the wounds that were nearly healed. "Oh my God, baby." They were all over my back, fifteen of them, and one in the front close to my heart. She stepped in front of me with tears in her eyes. "I'm so sorry. I didn't mean for all of those to happen. I didn't think it would get this far. I'm just..."

I dropped down in front of her and kissed her feet. "I love you, Jelissa. You are my church. There is no covenant without the shedding of blood. I am your sacrifice. Please just love me.

Please accept me. Please save me from this world, and myself. I am so lost and so flawed. Please save me. I need you. Please. I am broken, baby." Tears flowed down my cheeks.

I was worried that she would reject me. I was worried that she would snatch her love away from me. I was so tired of the pain. I was tired of being hurt and rejected. My injuries from my childhood still plagued me. The loss of my mother had my soul bound in a prison of pain. I needed release. I needed healing. I needed rescuing. I needed Jelissa Shantè.

She leaned over and helped me up. Her face was wet with tears. She held mine in her small hands and looked into my eyes. "Nobody has ever acted like they needed me before. You make me feel so different. So whole, so complete. I am so scared. Is this the right way to go? What about everybody else? I am still your brother's baby mother."

"I don't care. I love you. I need you. All I see is you. All I need is you. I am going to give you my all. I promise. Just give me you. Please."

She stood still for a moment just staring at me. Tears dripped off of her chin. "They gon' talk so much about us. They gon' call us names. They gon' say that we are bogus. They gon' turn their backs and throw a lot of stones. What will we do then? They will never understand us."

"But God will, and as long as He does, that's all that matters. You taught me that." I scooped her up and sucked all over her succulent lips. She leaned her head back. I kissed along her neck, and bit into it. She moaned louder. "I love you Jelissa Shantè. I love you, and I need you."

"I need you, too, T.J.. I swear, I need you too." She groaned. I laid her back on the bed and fell to my knees once again. This time, I spaced her knees and pulled her dress up her slender thighs. She arched her back. I could smell the scent of her perfume mixed with that of her arousal. Her kitty lips were shaven. They were puffy and slightly parted with a hint of gel seeping from in between them. I shivered and dove head first into her lap, my mouth vacuum sucking her sex ones. I slurped the juices and sought pleasure in the feel of her essence sliding down my throat. I peeled her petals apart and found her clitoris. My tongue traced quick circles around it repeatedly..

"Uhhhh, baby, shit!" She arched her back again and opened her knees further. "Mmm, baby, what are we doing?" I really went to work. My tongue tried to hit all of her pleasure spots at once. She wrapped her ankles around my head and proceeded to hump my face, moaning at the top of her lungs. "Ooo baby! Ooo, baby, we so wrong. We so wrong, but I love you so muchhhhhh!" She came stuffing my head further into her crotch.

I kept eating and licking. At the same as I knelt on the floor, I had my piece pulled out of my pants stroking it at full speed. I was so in need of her." She began to squirt all across my face and nose, before she pushed me away. I fell on to my elbows. She hopped off of the bed and took a hold of my piece. "Since we doing this then, let's do it. You are not in this alone. From here on out, it's you and me. I promise. That's my word as a woman."

She stroked my dick a few times before sucking the head into her mouth. She licked all around it and continued to pump it. She popped it out and looked me in the eyes. "The Bible says that the Lord will restore to you tenfold all that you have lost if you remain faithful to him, and seeing all of you, mmph." She smiled and sucked me back inside of her mouth going to work like a true Queen for her King.

I groaned and humped upward. My nails dug into my sides. It felt so good. I became more crazy about her. Even though we were together, I was missing her already. My emotions were all out of whack. I needed to be inside of her. I scooted back. She turned her head sideways and wiped her mouth. "What's the matter. You having second thoughts?"

"Hell n'all." I picked her up and placed her back on the bed. I dropped my pants completely and got between her thighs, lining myself up. I looked into her eyes again. "It's us, boo, for life. I got you. I would never enter you unless I was gon' be with you for life." I cocked back and slid home two inches at a time. The deeper I went the more she dug her nails into me. She came up and bit my neck hard. I groaned and shivered. "Do me, baby. Make me yours then."

That was all it took. I rolled my back, diving deep into that forbidden pussy. Stroke after stroke. She pulled me closer. "Hit it, baby! Come on! Hit it harder. Yesss! T.J." She groaned, biting my neck again.

I dove deeper and deeper as the bed bounced. My breathing became labored. Her cat was so tight and so juicy I feared I was going to cum too soon. "Awww, baby, deeper!" Her ankles wrapped around my waist and held me tighter while I pounded her out like a savage.

"Damn, baby girl. Damn! You feel so good. This shit so good. Awww, it's so good." I paused and told her to switch positions. I needed a moment. I was so close to cumming and we had only been going at it for ten minutes. I couldn't go out like that. Not on the first bout.

She bent over and spaced her knees. She looked back at me. "This time, please don't stop. We finish together. I know you needed a minute, it's okay. I'm yearin' for you, too. I love you T.J."

"I love you, too, baby girl." I slapped her ass and dove back in on straight beast mode. I took a hold of her hips and proceeded to hit that pussy hard. Our skins slapped into one another's, and she threw it back at me full force. I humped forward and plunged deeper as her walls sucked at me hungrily. My hand, on its own accord, began to slap that ass over and over.

"Uhhhh! Uhhhh! I'm gonna cum! I'm gonna cum!" She screamed. She lowered her head to the bed and forced her ass backwards harder and harder.

I couldn't take it anymore. I closed my eyes tightly and opened them just as her booty cheeks were jiggling. The sight of them, and her pretty toes bunched up was enough to send me over the edge. I came hard, my body convulsing behind her.

"Uhhhh, baby!" She shivered and bounced back into my lap again and again, milking me. Once she felt like all my seed had been released, she hopped on top of me and slid down my still throbbing piece and rode me to another orgasm while she wrapped her pretty hands around my neck, occasionally leaning down and licking along my it before she bit into it.

Before it was all said and done, we both came again, and spent ten minutes rubbing all over each other afterward. Both of us were misty eyed, lost within one another after knowing that we had crossed that final line. All I could say is that the feeling was beyond amazing, and when it was over and done with that night, she had me hooked and ready to do whatever for her. I had never felt more weak and strong at the same time.

CHAPTER 15
US AGAINST THE WORLD

He who finds a wife finds a good thing,
And obtains favor from the Lord.
	-Proverbs 18:22, NKJV

Month after month, Jelissa and I spent time together physically four times a week, for three and a half hours at a time. She sat next to me and took the time and patience to slowly walk me through the Bible. She helped me to gain a strong sense of knowledge of who I was as a man and how the world saw me, which didn't matter.

She took me through the scriptures and showed me how God saw me and the level of importance I had within his kingdom. The more she taught me, the harder I fell for her. Her intelligence, her kind heart, her sexiness, and the love that she had for me and my struggle, caused me to see life in a different light. I now understood that I was worthy to be loved. That I was not sentenced into eternal damnation because of my past or my blood line. She showed me I had a purpose in life. That I was worthy. She was my guiding light when there was nothing in my world but darkness and torment.

We got married at the prison within an intimate setting and immediately got baptized together. We were united under Christ. Though our struggles persisted, we clung to each other, and fell securely under the blood of the Father. Our persecutions became plentiful. Our families turned against us. We lost a lot of material things that set us backward. We lost friends that were at once so important and pivotal within our stability.

There were two more tries on my life that were unsuccessful, and the previous men that had stabbed me up the first time were found murdered within the prison. These were murders that the authorities tried to pin on me. Murders that I can't even go into detail about from fear of prosecution. All I can say is what goes around comes back around, and revenge is mine says the Lord.

※

Ahmad was charged with sexual assault of two minor girls shortly after me and Jelissa's ceremony. While inside, he sent two of his hit men to where he thought my wife's best friend's home was and they staked it out for three days straight. Luckily, her friend had moved away two days before they got there. If my wife would have been caught slipping, only God knows what would have taken place. He had her covered. Ahmad remains jaded, constantly plotting against us in the most devious of ways even to this day, but the Bible says that no weapons formed against His children shall prosper. He didn't say that they wouldn't be formed, he just said they would never prosper. I believe that to be the truth because so many had been formed against us and thus far, none of them have prospered.

Instead, Jelissa and I managed to come together, got on our grind to provide a life for our family. We wrote over a hundred novels that have done extremely well on the market. We have built a strong relationship with God and we seek first His

Kingdom above all else, and because we have been blessed beyond all measure we continue to bless so many others.

Our hearts, our souls, and our intentions remain pure and wholesome. We are still madly in love and insane about each other. I know without a shadow of a doubt, none of these feelings will ever change. While the road ahead promises to be challenging, we stand as one and we are prepared. With God leading the way, we will be just fine. I look forward to cherishing my wife and standing beside her through any and every obstacle that may present itself in front of us. We are one. Let no man separate what God has brought together.

NOTE FROM AUTHOR

I want to thank all of those who continue to support my wife and I as we continue on this new journey. Thank you all for supporting our love. We've been through some challenging things, but our love has allowed us to overcome them all.

As a man, it is my job to secure the stability of her and our children. Thank you for giving us a chance; for every download, every share, every review, etc.

Please be sure to join our reading group !
https://www.facebook.com/groups/tjpreaderz/

Peace and love, T.J.

Check out a sneak peek of Jelissa Shante's newest novel, A Love Worth The Wait: My Journey As A Prison Wife...

PROLOGUE

Ever had a moment when the boogeyman was realer than you thought? He'd come and go. Just as you'd start to trust your surroundings, he'd pop up out of nowhere, sometimes he was closer to home than you knew.

I was excited to see him. It'd been a while since I'd seen him. He'd been away for about eight years. My mother had did my hair the night before. I could barely sleep that night.
Today's the day, Jelissa. Two o'clock.
I had worn a blue jean skirt, a canary colored long-sleeved shirt paired with my black Mary Janes. I had to wear the white girly socks with the silk-like ruffles. Hated them. Those damn things always made my ankles itch, but my mother wasn't having it. A child was always supposed to dress like that; a child.
I grabbed my pink purse filled with my mini Polly Pocket sets, so I'd have something to keep me entertained, checked to ensure I had my money, nothing but three one-dollar bills and a gang of coins. I had also had a pack of Winterfresh gum along with the nasty red Peppermint candies my grandma always gave me during Sunday service. I didn't

know if it was my breath or her trying to suppress my appetite, either way, I hated the candy and still do to this day.

I retrieved my green candy apple roll-on lip gloss from my purse and applied some to my dry lips. I never really liked wearing lip gloss because I always wound up licking it all off my lips before the day was over. Plus, I'd been counting down the days 'til this very moment. Pop!

One o'clock.

I was ready early. I couldn't contain my excitement. I grabbed my spring jacket, put it on and went to the front room. I stood in the window waiting. Waiting for the silver Honda Civic.

Two o'clock. A smile crept across my chestnut colored face. I Popped my lips together to make sure they were still glossy and smooth.

Three o'clock.

May be he was stuck in traffic.

"His car isn't out there yet?" My mother questioned.

"No," I replied, my smile slowly fading.

"He said he'd be pulling up soon."

"Okay." My smile returned. He was late, but I missed him so much. Last year before this, I was only seeing him once a week for three hours at a time. My grandmother made the long drive consistently. My whole world would light up at seeing him, just for it to be crushed when he had to walk back through the gray metal door.

Four o'clock.

My knees started to give out on me as I stood at the bay window. My breath fogging up the area in which my face could reach.

Five o'clock.

A silver Honda Civic drove past, turned around and parked across the street from my house. Finally. The car door opened, but it wasn't him. All the life in me had left.

Six o'clock.

"What do you mean you're not coming, Darnell?" I overheard my mother on the phone. "She's been waiting in that window since one o'clock. It's not fair to her. You told her you were coming. I'm not going to allow you to keep doing this to my daughter, having her sitting here looking *crazy waiting on you. Don't make promises you can't keep."* With that she hung up. *"He's not coming, Jelissa. I'm sorry."*

I dragged my feet as I walked back to my room, leaving the light off. I took everything off and got into my bed. I cried myself to sleep that night. Is there something I did wrong? What was wrong with me? Why wasn't I good enough? Why couldn't he keep his promises to me? I thought. This had been the twelfth time he'd stood me up.

At seven-years-old, that's when I had experienced my first real heartbreak. A father was supposed to be a girl's first hero, her first true love. His job was to show her how she was supposed to be treated by how he treated her. I didn't experience none of that. I had waited eight years for this man to get home, envisioning the bond we'd have, but it was nothing like what I thought it'd be.

My father was in and out of my life, all of my life, yet I still had hope he'd come to fully love me and commit to playing an active role in my life. He was the king of habitual lies and false promises. But the times he did come through, he'd spoil me with clothes, jewelry, shoes, etc. just to disappear for another few weeks to a month at a time.

Six years later, the same man I trusted time and time again, shattered me. My life had been full of hurt and disappointment since age seven. My mother did all she could to protect me, to nurture me, to be the best mother she knew how to be, raising three kids on her own with minimal help. I bet her world come crashing down if she knew the pain her first born had carried for twenty-nine years.

We're always expected to cope with things, but never taught how to heal.

Little did I know, in the years to come, all of the trauma I'd went through would cause me to go looking for love in all the wrong places just to fill the void; the hole in my heart. I wore my heart on my sleeve. Accepting whatever came my way just to feel loved. To feel cared for. A broken girl looking to be good enough for *somebody*.

I just didn't know that Jelissa would never be the same. So, I grabbed my notebook and pen and just wrote.

Love is painful and has brought nothing but sorrow

I've spent countless nights crying no longer looking forward to tomorrow

The lies, the excuses, I've taken everything, even the back seat

Why do I insist on being in a relationship when I still feel incomplete?

The pain stings and my eyes burn

Do lessons come in the form of tears, what if any, shall I learn?

Lord, I'm begging you to open my eyes

Open them; give me the ability to see

That healthy love is obtainable

But first I have to learn to love me

-Jelissa

CHAPTER 1
NO ANGEL

Oh, you see that skin?
It's the same she's been standing in
Since the day she saw him walking away
Now she's left cleaning up the mess he made
So fathers, be good to your daughters
Daughters will love like you do
Girls become lovers who turn into mothers
So mothers be good to your daughters, too

"You just lil' Miss Perfect, aren't chu? You can't ever do no wrong. What; you think you better than everybody, Lil' Miss Perfect? Well, you ain't. And you can't have him. You can't have my father. He's mine! Not yours. You got yo' own father. You get everything. I swear, I hate chu!"

Renee had always been the type of person who created things in her own head. She saw what made sense to her rather than what was actually taking place. No, I never thought I was perfect, nor did I ever think I was better than anyone. True; I had my *own* father. But his ass was clearly confused on the role he played in my life; thinking he was my man as opposed to being my father.

He couldn't stand the mere thought of me having another male role model in my life, though. One who I called dad. My stepfather. One who gave me unconditional love and didn't expect anything from me in return, unlike himself.

My *father*, and I use that term loosely, had purchased me my first cell phone at the age of twelve to keep tabs on me. Monitoring my calls. You may say, *Jelissa, that's what parents are supposed to do*. Um, no! He did way too much. Disconnecting my phone when he was upset with me. Comparing himself to the boys I crushed on in Jr. High. *"Why you tell them young niggas you love them, but you don't say that to me? They don't love you. You kiss on them, but you don't want to kiss me? I don't understand you, Leesee."* Right; I bet he didn't. He never really tried to understand me. He was too busy expecting shit from me I couldn't give, knowing damn well he barely played an active role in my life.

My sister didn't know the half. Didn't know a damn thing about what her *perfect* sister was going through right under her nose. Bet she had no clue what happened in that bathroom at the sitter's house, for three years. Every Monday through Friday like clockwork. Right around nap time, her *perfect* seven-year-old sister was forced to put her head between some sixteen year's old legs or play with some five-year-old's penis while all the other kids caught z's.

So what, I was an honor roll student with nothing but A's and B's. I was shocked that I'd still been able to maintain my impressive academic progress while being subjected to the madness. But *perfect*; no. I was far from it.

She didn't know that the real reason I grew to love the sounds of jazz music at night was to evade my nightmares. And totally oblivious to the fact that most nights, my pillow soaked up the gut-wrenching sobs that tore through my nine-year-old chest, hoping, damn near praying, I'd die in my sleep. If only Renee knew the overwhelming pressure I was under.

It's easy to say, *"Jelissa, why didn't you speak up? Why didn't you say something?"* Ask the millions of victims of sexual assaults who are now broken adults that same question, then I'll provide you with my answer. I had no safe place. I felt alone.

But once my siblings and I aged out of the sitter's home, well, once I was old enough to babysit myself, I thought my worries were over, until my sperm donor's obvious remarks of hitting on me became more apparent in my teen years.

During my teenage years, I became more rebellious and acted out. My mother caught me up in some mess I had no business doing, which resulted in me being put out of her home and forced to live with my *father*.

He became too comfortable with me being in his home. Walking in on me half naked. Showing me extra love and affection. Referring to me by my childhood nickname, thinking that would soften me. Not knowing, I still carried the painful burden of his inconsistent presence in my life up into my teens.

During my stay at his home is when he made his first move while we were alone, but soon after many failed attempts and my threat to tell someone, he got the hint. Eventually, I found ways to never be left alone with him and I started to treat him accordingly. Dealt with him on my terms. Using him like he used me.

So no, *sis*, I didn't want your father. I didn't want to overstep my boundaries nor ever make you feel as though you were competing. I just wanted what I always felt like you took for granted.

I'll never have the opportunity to go to a father-daughter dance, but you'll be able to tell all about it. I can count on one hand, matter fact, two fingers, how many graduations or school functions of mine my father has been to, but you'll never know about that. You see, you never had those issues. Your father made his presence know.

The only thing I learned from my *father* was how to lie so much you start to believe your own bullshit, and how amazingly pleasurable sex could be. I took no joy in the act itself, but the orgasms from the oral he gave me was deniable. Every fiber of my being knew it was wrong, but my body betrayed me. How could I stop? How could I stop him? Who would believe me if I told?

But here I was, still broken. Still damaged. Hell, I wanted love. In fact, I needed love. Craved it. Yearned for it. For once, I wanted to experience what you had all these years, sis. You may not have always gotten your way, but one thing you'll never be able to say is that your father wasn't there. While you were sitting there rehearsing the lyrics to Beyonce's, *Daddy* to lip-sing to your father, I was sitting in the window or by the door simply praying mine would show up, eventually.

www.ingramcontent.com/pod-product-compliance
Lightning Source LLC
Chambersburg PA
CBHW061455040426
42450CB00007B/1371